AID AS OBSTACLE

Twenty Questions about our Foreign Aid and the Hungry

AID AS OBSTACLE

Twenty Questions about our Foreign Aid and the Hungry

FRANCES MOORE LAPPE
JOSEPH COLLINS
DAVID KINLEY

INSTITUTE FOR FOOD
AND DEVELOPMENT POLICY
1885 MISSION ST., SAN FRANCISCO, CA 94103 USA

To order additional copies of this book, please write:

Institute for Food and Development Policy
1885 Mission St.
San Francisco, CA 94103 USA
(415) 864-8555

Please add 15 percent for postage and handling ($1 minimum).
Bulk discounts available.

Distributed in the United Kingdom by:

Third World Publications
151 Stratford Rd.
Birmingham B11 1RD
England

Design: Ellen Oberzil-Leishman
Type: Good Times Graphics
Printers: McNaughton & Gunn, Ann Arbor
Text: Times Roman

ACKNOWLEDGEMENTS

This book reflects the help of many friends and colleagues around the world. First we wish to thank all our colleagues at the Institute for Food and Development Policy. In addition, we would like to offer special thanks to Tony Jackson, James Boyce, Betsy Hartmann, Tomasson Januzzi, Guy Gran, Jay Steptoe, Robert Ayres, Bereket Selassie, Michael Klare, Michael Moffitt, Ben Stavis, Dan Lindheim, Steve Hellinger, Garreth Porter, Stephen Minkin, Joel Rocamora, Walden Bello, Gail Omvedt, Ho Kwon Ping, Blythe Reis, Alan Taylor, Peggy Barlett, Larry Simon, Susan McCord, Cheryl Payer, Bill Rau, Michael Sinkay, Kathleen Gough, field staff of the Mennonite Central Committee, field staff of the Catholic Relief Service, Bill Ellis, Ernest Feder, Jim Morrell, Fay Bennett Watts, Stephen Commins, Tim Atwater, A.J.M. van de Laar, the Data Center, Robert Anderson, Sheldon Geller, Tony Phillips, Philip Berryman, Robert Gersony, Jo Froman, Mary Jean Haley, Richard Franke, Barbara Chasin, Anne-Marie Holenstein, Peter Hayes, Hannes Lorenzen, Jun Atienza, Michael Scott, and Michael Watts.

We are grateful for the typing assistance of Ina Moore, Luanne Rowder and Lisa Kokin. We thank Doug Basinger for his fine editorial and production assistance and Patty Somlo for her help in proofreading.

We appreciate the many contributions from individuals, churches and foundations that make the Institute's work possible. A list of current contributors to the Institute may be found at the end of this book.

TABLE OF CONTENTS

INTRODUCTION

Writing this book turned out to be more than the challenge of assessing the impact of U.S. foreign aid for we were forced to confront such difficult questions as: What causes poverty and hunger? What is development? Who can bring about development? What responsibilities do Americans have in a world of needless suffering? In this Introduction we seek to capsulize our understanding of these fundamental issues.

Is more aid the answer?

"They are poor and hungry. We in the United States have so much. Shouldn't we increase our foreign aid?"

This is the natural response of many Americans when confronted by the incredible deprivation in which most of the world's people are forced to live.

This understandable response of wanting to give to the needy is reinforced by foreign aid policymakers. In 1980, a special Presidential Commission on World Hunger recommended a tripling of the percentage of the U.S. gross national product devoted to foreign aid. About the same time, an independent international commission, initiated by World Bank President Robert McNamara and headed by former West German Chancellor Willy Brandt, called for massive increases in industrial countries' foreign aid.

By the time these commissions made their recommendations, the Carter administration had already committed U.S. taxpayers to more foreign aid than ever—over $8 billion in fiscal 1980—to be channeled through the Agency for International Development,† food aid programs,† the World Bank,† and other multilateral aid agencies.† American taxpayers were asked to virtually double their contribution to the World Bank, the leading source of development loans.

Justifying their programs, aid spokespersons assure us that strategies for development have dramatically improved, and that emphasis on rapid industrialization and the "green revolution" has been discarded in favor of a new development strategy. The new

---

† See "A Primer: Some Essential Facts about the Aid Establishment" at the end of this book for an in-depth description. Throughout the entire book, this symbol † will be used to denote terms included in the "Primer."

"basic human needs"† approach, we are told, directly focuses on the poor—the productivity of small farms, small-scale technology, and infrastructure that will help the entire rural population in third world countries.

U.S. aid policymakers testify that they follow the "new directions"† reforms mandated by Congress. According to former Secretary of State Cyrus Vance, the principal purpose of U.S. development assistance programs is "to meet the basic needs of the poor people in the developing countries." Since most of the world's nearly one billion underfed people live in rural areas, aid is now directed, we are told, to agriculture and rural development. It is also claimed that food aid programs are also designed to directly benefit the poor and contribute toward self-sufficiency. We are assured, moreover, that U.S. aid has been linked to human rights in recipient countries to encourage more democracy and less repression.

Appropriate terminology?

Along with the "new directions" thrust of major U.S.-funded aid programs has come catchy new terminology to describe it. Today, we hear much about "integrated rural development," "appropriate technology," "popular participation," "raising small farm productivity" and "self-reliance." But whatever the terminology, our foreign assistance programs will help the poor and hungry abroad only if they attack the root causes of their suffering. Since "root causes" has itself become a popular phrase—sometimes used glibly—we must be very precise about what we mean.

Our research at the Institute for Food and Development Policy leads us to conclude that the cause of hunger and rural poverty is *not* overpopulation, scarcity of agricultural resources, or lack of modern technology. Rather, *the root cause of hunger is the increasing concentration of control over food-producing resources in the hands of fewer and fewer people.* Privileged elites preempt control over food-producing resources for their own benefit. No new combination of material inputs, no matter how "appropriate," can address the powerlessness of the poor that is at the root of hunger. (We document these findings in detail in our book *Food First: Beyond the Myth of Scarcity* (Ballantine Books, 1979).)

Aid reinforces power relationships

Field investigations and other research have led us to realize that U.S. foreign assistance fails to help the poor because it is *of necessity* based on one fundamental fallacy: that aid can reach the powerless even though channeled through the powerful. Official foreign assistance necessarily flows through the recipient governments, and too often (particularly in those countries to which the United States confines most of its aid) these governments represent narrow, elite economic interests. We have learned that additional material resources are usually not needed to eliminate hunger. In fact, the influx of such outside resources into those countries where economic control is concentrated in the hands of a few bolsters the local, national and international elites whose stranglehold over land and other productive resources generates poverty and hunger in the first place. Instead of helping, we *hurt* the dispossessed majority.

Tubewells designed to benefit the poorest farmers in a Bangladesh village become the property of the village's richest landlord; food-for-work projects in Haiti intended to help the landless poor end up as a boon to the village elite; rural electrification justified as a prerequisite to jobs in rural industries results in the elimination of jobs for thousands of poor rural women in Indonesia.

Foreign aid, we have found, has not transformed antidemocratic economic control by a few into a participatory, democratic process of change. It cannot. Rather, official foreign aid *reinforces* the power relationships that already exist. Certainly this is the case with government-to-government aid. Only with great difficulty can private ("voluntary") agencies† sometimes avoid the same dynamics.

Aid policymakers claim that they are now focusing on the poorest countries and on those governments demonstrating commitment to the poor. In this book we challenge both claims. Our research shows instead that the bulk of our aid flows not to the countries with the greatest poverty, but to those with some of the world's most narrowly based and repressive regimes. We challenge the claim that most new aid projects target poor people. Most funds actually go to large-scale infrastructural projects benefitting the better-off people who control land and marketing systems and have political influence. Finally, we contend that even the few projects which do promote the productivity of small farmers (and perhaps boost their productivity), still fail to address the real sources of their poverty. Moreover, such projects hurt the poor rural majority—the landless and nearlandless.

Lack of resources or lack of power?

Some might interpret us to be saying that the aid establishment is not living up to its rhetoric. But that is only part, and not the most important part, of what we are saying. What we are saying is that U.S. government aid and agencies such as the World Bank cannot ally themselves with the poor, in part because the definition of the problem of poverty reflected in their projects is wrong.

The prevailing diagnosis of why people are poor and hungry is that they have been "left out" of the development process. From this diagnosis flows one solution—bring the poor *into* development. "Basic needs" aid strategies are conceived as a way to widen the development process to include the poor. But such a diagnosis is simply another version of the fallacious theory that one can reach the poor by expanding a process controlled by the rich.

A very different diagnosis is that rather than being *left out* of the development process, the poor have been an integral part of the process—both as resource and as victim. The poor have provided their labor, their products and often their land. The issue, then, is not to bring the poor into the development process, but for the poor to achieve the power they need to direct a development process in their interests.

The official aid agencies' diagnosis is that the poor are poor because they lack certain things— irrigation, credit, better seeds, good roads, etc. But we ask: *Why* are they lacking these things? In studying country after country, it becomes clear that what the poor really lack is *power,* power to secure what they need. The aid agencies focus on the lack of materials; we focus on the lack of power. Therein lies the fundamental difference.

By identifying the problem as a lack of resources, official aid seeks to bring in what is lacking locally. We have found that not only are the needed resources often available locally, but also that the outside resources—brought in by official aid—invariably end up in the hands of elites who are then even better able to usurp the labor and dwindling resources of the poor majority.

The official diagnosis assumes that the poor are living in a static condition of backwardness and that the role of aid is to offer material incentives and benevolent prods to get things moving. But in countries where so many people are poor and hungry, the reality in the villages and in the nation is this: if positive change is not already under way, it is because of people's legitimate fear of those more powerful and because of the constraints on production built into hierarchical, often quasi-feudal social structures.

While prevailing development theory sees stagnation and backwardness in third world countries, the truth is that in every country where many are poor and hungry, people are working to achieve genuine development, beginning with redistribution of control over land. To some, their efforts appear insignificant in light of the mighty forces against them. But recall that many observers belittled the freedom movements in the African Portuguese colonies as late as the early 1970s, and those of the Nicaraguan people as late as 1979. Likewise, observing the suffering of so many Chinese in the 1940s, knowledgeable Americans suggested that a high death rate in China might be humane, since the country could never feed itself. Who would say that today?

With all the obstacles they face, these societies and others serve to highlight the most important lesson of development—the need to first address the question of control over productive resources.

In formulating a definition of development that puts us on the side of the poor, we have had to distinguish development from "productivity." We have learned that it is possible to have more of both while, at the same time, the poor majority become poorer and more desperate for survival. Genuine development necessarily involves changes in relationships among people and in their power to control productive resources. Development is a *social* process in which people join together to build economic and political institutions serving the interests of the majority. In that process, more and more people unite to acquire the knowledge and techniques they need to develop their resources and free themselves from needless hunger, disease and ignorance.

Why a push for more aid?

To ally themselves with the interests of the poor, agencies such as U.S. AID would have to support those groups throughout the third world that are confronting the issue of power—the issue of control over resources. To do so would pit these agencies against the interests of the elites dominating most governments in the world today. To do so would go headlong against the formidable lobbyists of multinational corporations. To do so would be to risk supporting democratic economic alternatives abroad that might lead more Americans to question how just their own economic system has become. Obviously, no U.S. government agency is about to do so. This is why we conclude that agencies of the U.S. government are incapable of arriving at a correct diagnosis of the root causes of hunger—a diagnosis that puts control over resources in the central position.

The promotion of the wrong diagnosis permits many well-intentioned persons (including some within aid agencies) to be used by the real beneficiaries of foreign aid—multinational corporations and their third world partners—who are the most trenchant lobbyists for foreign aid.

The role of outsiders

From these contrasting analyses of the problem of hunger and poverty flow very different roles for the outsider. Our government tells us that the appropriate role for the United States is to supply needed resources and help maintain "stability" in the third world. Mounting economic and military aid to countries like the Philippines and El Salvador is so justified. But if progress will come only with redistribution of control over productive resources, then outside interventions to maintain "stability" will only postpone the day when necessary progress can begin. Moreover, by bolstering the forces that block change, outside support makes brutal and bloody confrontations even more inevitable.

Our definition of the problem leads to a very different challenge to those outside the third world. We should not try to make our aid agencies live up to their new rhetoric. This would only contribute to the problem by reinforcing the notion that U.S. foreign aid can help in countries where control over resources is tightly concentrated. Once we understand that government-to-government aid cannot transform power relationships, but can only reinforce what exists, it becomes clear that we must work to limit such aid to countries where there is *already* under way a fundamental restructuring of decision-making power.

Remove the obstacles

Many who have called for a halt or reduction in U.S. foreign aid have actually been saying, "Cut them off. Let them solve their own problems. We must take care of our own." This is *not* what we are saying. Rather, we are calling for a halt to all economic and military support for governments controlled by narrowly based elites which use repression to protect their interests and to block the demands of their own people for redistribution of control over productive assets. Such a move would mean cutting off those governments now most favored by U.S. economic assistance and military aid. The thesis of this book is that these economic and military supports actually block efforts by those who are working for a more just sharing of control over resources. As Americans, our responsibility is to remove such obstacles. At the same time we must work to make our own society truly democratic and self-reliant so that one day it might play a constructive role around the world.

1

QUESTION

Do U.S. aid programs focus on countries where poverty is worst?

RESPONSE Before tackling this
question—where
aid flows—we must first determine for what purposes our
bilateral aid† dollars are officially
designated. Of the entire $5.6 bil-
lion request for aid appropriations for fiscal year (FY) 1980,*
only *one quarter* is allocated to
what AID calls development proj-
ects.¹ What happens to the vast
bulk of our aid dollars? Our entire book tries to answer that
question. Suffice it here to state
the programs under which our aid
dollars flow. One third goes to the
Economic Support Fund† (also
known as Security Supporting
Assistance†), one quarter goes to
food aid, and the remainder goes
to international organizations,
operating expenses of AID, and
the Peace Corps.²

The hidden third of AID

In other words, the biggest
single chunk of our bilateral aid
dollars—namely, one third—goes
to the Economic Support Fund, a
program which most Americans
have never even heard of. According to congressional legislation, the Economic Support Fund
"provides balance of payments,
infrastructure and other capital
and technical assistance to
regions of the world in which the
United States has special foreign
policy and security interests."³

The Economic Support Fund is
disbursed as grants rather than
loans and without the slightest
reference to poverty criteria or its
impact on the poor. Eighty-six
percent of the Economic Support
Fund proposed for FY 1980 is
allocated to the Middle East.
Egypt and Israel alone receive 77
percent. Through the Economic
Support Fund these two countries
would receive more than all development projects funded by AID
anywhere in the world.⁴

In Egypt, in FY 1979, $750 mil-
lion from the Economic Support
Fund was used for a new telecommunications network (slated to
swallow $3 billion in AID funds
over seven years), highways, "agribusiness development," and
agricultural mechanization ($17
million in tractors alone even
though tractors are likely to dis-
place jobs needed by the one-

---

† See "A Primer: Some Essential Facts about the Aid Establishment" at the end of this
book for an in-depth description. Throughout the entire book, this symbol † will be
used to denote terms included in the "Primer."

* As of this writing it is still not clear whether or not FY 1980 appropriations will be approved. Analyzing FY 1979 appropriations or the proposed appropriations for FY
1981, however, does not reveal a substantially different pattern of aid distribution.

Tarbela, Pakistan, man at cattle fair.

third of all rural families who are landless). At least $300 million of one year's aid to Israel is spent without any accounting at all to the U.S. government, according to a statement made by the AID administrator in FY 1978 congressional hearings.[5]

To the poorest countries?

AID claims that, in FY 1980, 90 percent of its "development assistance" (this excludes the Economic Support Fund, food aid, and the Peace Corps) goes to the poorest developing countries.[6]

We did our own calculations of the portion going to the poorest countries. Taking the list of countries that AID labels "low-income" in the very same book making the 90 percent claim, we find that not 90 percent but 32 percent of development assistance goes to low-income countries.[7] If we include the Economic Support Fund, food aid, and the Peace Corps (which we believe gives a much fairer picture of where our aid dollars go), we discover that only 21 percent of our aid dollars go to low-income countries.

How could this be? How could AID claim that 90 percent goes to poorest countries? We finally figured out what AID was doing. AID simply found a definition of "low-income" that fit its purposes. In small print under the chart making the 90 percent claim, AID notes that the definition of low-income used for the chart is the one used by the International Development Association (IDA)† to determine eligibility for its loans. IDA considers eligible all countries with a $580 per capita GNP or less—a limit almost *twice* as high as that most

commonly used to define the poorest countries.[8] Using this much looser criterion almost doubles the list of "poorest countries" from 39 to 72. If this broader IDA loan eligibility criterion is used, then three-quarters of the 55 countries receiving AID development assistance in the FY 1980 budget can be labeled as "poorest." Applying the most widely accepted definition of the poorest countries, however, less than half of the recipients of U.S. development assistance are among the poorest.

AID's focus

While not focused on the poorest countries, our aid dollars certainly are focused. About that there is no dispute. Of the bilateral economic assistance going to 34 low-income countries, only four—India, Bangladesh, Indonesia and Pakistan—are allocated almost two-thirds of the total.[9]

Of the almost 100 countries that receive aid from AID, only 10 receive over half of all bilateral economic assistance in FY 1980 appropriations requests. (Please refer to Chart I. Note that three of the top recipients of our aid dollars—Israel, Turkey and Portugal—aren't even third world countries. Also note that three Middle East countries capture one-third of the total.)

Yes, our aid dollars are focused. They are concentrated in those countries which the U.S. administration identifies as being of strategic importance.

CHART I

Ten Top Recipients Get 51 Percent of U.S. Bilateral Economic Assistance* ($ millions proposed, FY 1980)

1. Egypt	**$969.6**
2. Israel	**786.0**
3. India**	**245.5**
4. Indonesia**	**205.0**
5. Bangladesh**	**184.1**
6. Turkey	**98.8**
7. Portugal	**90.0**
8. Pakistan**	**86.9**
9. Philippines	**83.3**
10. Syria	**65.5**

Ten Top Recipients:	**$2,814.7**
Approximately 90 Others:	**2,739.4**
Total Economic Assistance:	**$5,554.1**

Portion going to development projects (called Functional Development Assistance and Sahel Programs):   26 percent

---

* Includes Development Assistance, Economic Support Fund, Food Aid, Peace Corps and International Narcotics Control
** "low-income" World Bank definition

2

QUESTION

If U.S. aid does not go to the poorest countries, does it at least focus on those countries where governments have shown a commitment to help the poor?

RESPONSE Glance again at Chart I. You'll find that of the 10 top recipients of U.S. economic assistance, excluding the Middle East allies, only five are third world countries. These countries—India, Indonesia, Bangladesh, Pakistan and the Philippines—are hardly known for their commitment to addressing the needs of the poor. At least four—Indonesia, Bangladesh, the Philippines, and Pakistan—have earned international reputations both for their neglect of the needs of the poor and for their repression of those working for change.[1]

Indonesia. The nutritional status of a large portion of Indonesians is steadily deteriorating.[2] According to the World Bank, close to one-third of the children in Indonesia under the age of five (about seven million children) suffer from moderate to severe protein-calorie malnutrition.[3] Part of the reason for this deterioration is that by 1973, almost half of Java's rural households (more than 30 million people) were virtually landless, according to the United Nations International Labor Office.[4] This figure does not include smallholders and tenant farmers "who have been reduced to de facto landless laborers through the modernization of rice production." In 1979, riots over land ownership were quelled by government troops.[5]

The Suharto dictatorship nevertheless has blocked agrarian reform. Instead, it squanders the nation's spectacular oil and gas export revenues ($10 billion in 1979) on luxury imports, military excesses and showy capital-intensive industrial projects that neither provide for the needs of the majority nor generate employment for a country in which at least half of the labor force is either unemployed or underemployed.[6]

When a government causes such suffering, the only way it can remain in power is through repression. Indonesia's military dictatorship may well hold the record for the greatest number of long-term political prisoners. Authoritatively estimated to number 100,000 in 1977, most of the prisoners have been held since the 1965 military coup.[7]

If the Indonesian government refuses to use its sizable foreign exchange earnings from oil exports to benefit the poor, why would another $186 million from

U.S. taxpayers put into the same hands be expected to help?

Pakistan. Amnesty International estimates that the harsh martial law regime of General Zia-ul-Haq is holding 7,000 opponents and "perhaps many more" in prison. Journalists, industrial and rural labor organizers, lawyers, and former ministers and members of national and provincial assemblies have been imprisoned for their "participation in peaceful political activities."[8] Their trials, if they were even tried, were held in kangaroo courts (with no right to defense lawyers). In addition to imprisonment, many were stripped and flogged.[9] The army has brutally intervened on the side of the landowners in numerous landlord-laborer conflicts and has systematically repressed ethnic minorities in the poorest border region.[10]

The heavily aid-promoted and government-subsidized introduction of high technology farming has exacerbated the inequities in the countryside.[11] The distribution of income, which improved somewhat in the 1960s, became less equitable in the 1970s.[12] Nominal land reforms have had little impact and official figures indicate that eight percent of the farms use at least 42 percent of the farmland, mostly prime

Sugar mill, Negros Island, the Philippines.

land.[13] Forty percent of the general population, mainly in rural areas, is thought to be undernourished.[14] Infant mortality, estimated at 113 per 1,000 live births, is higher than in other South Asian countries.[15]

In 1977, Pakistan spent only one percent of its GNP on health commerce would like to see greater investment in "modernizing" agriculture (because they would benefit), the government, as in Indonesia, must give priority to "internal security" in order to defend the social status quo. The government's expenditure on agricultural development, there-

Six top recipients of U.S. economic aid are also top recipients of military assistance.

services (mostly in urban areas), compared to a two and one-half percent average for all third world countries. The number of doctors has fallen by about 20 percent over the past 10 years.[16] In education, the government's elite bias is clear: in 1977, it spent only one-third of the third world country average expenditure on primary education but spent at a level comparable to other countries for university-level education. In 1977, only 16 percent of the male population and two percent of the female population could read and write.[17]

Bangladesh. In this country of exceptional agricultural potential, well over half the population is chronically underfed.[18] Yet the military rulers allocate almost as much of the national budget to internal security (defense, police and "justice") as to agricultural development.[19] Even though the elites who control the land and fore, increased only five percent in real terms between 1972 and 1977.[20]

The Philippines. During the first five years after Ferdinand Marcos imposed martial law in 1972, AID loans and grants lept fivefold. At the same time, worldwide AID loans and grants increased only 25 percent.[21]

Since 1972, the wealth and power of the ruling clique surrounding Marcos has continued to swell while the real income and nutrition of workers and peasants have steadily declined.[22] By 1978, the nation's per capita calorie consumption had fallen to the *lowest in all Asia*, war-devastated Cambodia being the tragic exception.[23] Strikes are banned and union organizing is outlawed in key industries and in agriculture. Thousands of Filipinos have been imprisoned for opposing the dictatorship, and many have been tortured and killed.[24]

Land reform was proclaimed by Marcos as the cornerstone of the "new society" in 1972. But at its current pace, one economist has calculated that "it will take nearly 1,000 years for the cornerstone to be laid and cemented."[25] After seven years only one tenant in 200 among those that the land reform was supposed to help has received full ownership title. Additionally, many tenants and all the landless were excluded from the scope of the reform from its inception. In fact, largely because of the expansion of export crops by large growers and multinational firms, land ownership in the Philippines is growing more concentrated, not less.[26] The government's commitment to agrarian reform is reflected in its 1980 budget: the appropriation for agrarian reform is only six percent of the "defense" appropriation.[27]

Blind to this reality, many of AID's agricultural schemes are premised upon the successful implementation of Marcos' land reform. In 1979, moreover, the Carter administration reached an agreement with Marcos for a vast escalation in U.S. aid. The U.S. government agreed to provide $300 million in military aid and credit sales along with over $1 billion in economic aid over the next five years.[28] The military aid, say U.S. policymakers, is in exchange for the continued American use of Clark Air and Subic Naval bases. Such military aid, however, will be used not to defend the Philippines from external attack but against the growing number of Filipinos, including two armed resistance movements, attempting to overthrow the oppressive dictatorship.[29]

India. On the surface India might seem to contrast with these four other leading recipients of U.S. aid that are repressive military dictatorships. With the exception of the "emergency" imposed by Mrs. Ghandi, the country has seemingly preserved a system of parliamentary democracy. Yet maintaining a formal democracy—one given to the rhetoric of economic justice while inequalities in control over resources grow more extreme—has provided little consolation for the country's poor majority.

In the three decades since independence, India has received massive amounts of aid from both the East and the West. But the small and marginal farmers and the landless have not benefited. Agricultural programs have helped the rural elites to "modernize," providing them incentives to push tenants and small farmers off the land. As a result, the rate of increase of people deprived of land has been almost double the rate of population growth since the 1950s.[31] Recently the government revealed that 48 percent of the rural people and 41 percent of the urban people fall below minimal standards of nutritional intake.[32]

According to an AID-contracted study, land reform legislation has not only failed to fulfill its objectives but has hurt the small

Fertilizer factory, Lahore, Pakistan, financed by the World Bank.

tenants and sharecroppers. The reform has been a dismal failure, according to the study: "Neither the political authorities nor the legal institutions such as the judiciary have paid much heed to the needs of the small cultivators and landless workers."[33]

In many parts of the country where the poor try to organize, they are threatened, beaten or even murdered by local police and hired thugs who work for the landlords and rich farmers.

The direction of the last three decades does not seem to be changing. Nor is it questioned.

War against poverty or against the poor?

The linking of "development" aid with military aid to the Philippines is not an exception. Six top recipients of U.S. economic aid are also top recipients of military assistance. (See Chart II.) In addition, U.S. military assistance and government-arranged sales to underdeveloped countries amount to more than *four times* the total of all project aid through AID.[34] At least eight of the recipients of military aid from the Carter administration (Brazil, Indonesia, Argentina, South Korea, Nicaragua [under Somoza], the Philippines, Thailand and Bangladesh) have been designated by the U.S. Department of State as "gross violators of human rights."[35]

Americans are encouraged by U.S. policymakers to see development aid and military aid as unrelated. But genuine development requires that the poor and their allies organize to achieve a more equitable sharing in control over resources. It is precisely such popular efforts that our military aid helps to suppress.

CHART II

Ten Top Recipients Get 90 Percent of U.S. Military Assistance ($ millions proposed, FY 1981)

1. Israel	**$1,000.0**
2. Egypt	**551.0**
3. Turkey	**252.0**
4. Greece	**182.7**
5. South Korea	**176.5**
6. Spain	**125.6**
7. Philippines	**75.7**
8. Portugal	**75.7**
9. Jordan	**52.7**
10. Thailand	**51.4**

Types of assistance:	Ten Top recipients:	**$2,720.8**
Foreign Military Sales (FMS) **$2,840.0**	All other recipients:	**286.7**
Military Assistance Program (MAP) **$135.0**		
International Military Education and Training Program (IMET) **$32.5**	Total military assistance:	**$3,007.5**

Source: Congressional Presentation, Department of Defense

3

Doesn't our economic aid have a moderating influence on a repressive foreign government? A cutoff of U.S. aid would appear to doubly punish the poor who live under a repressive regime.

RESPONSE Unfortunately, history teaches us that this rationale for continuing aid is based on a fallacy—that U.S. official aid can promote economic advances for the poor where political rights are systematically denied. It cannot.

The plight of the poor majority in a country like Indonesia, a major recipient of U.S. aid, confirms this fact. Even the *Wall Street Journal* notes that an economic advance for Indonesia's poor depends on a "realignment of power in the villages."[1] This is unlikely to happen, notes the *Journal*, as long as "the government won't even allow the landless to organize pressure groups." Political rights and economic rights cannot be seen as distinct.

Moreover, we must never lose sight of the fact that the very government that denies people both economic assets and political rights and violates their human rights is also the government that aid officials *must* collaborate with if they want to operate in that country. As well as giving material support, official aid gives that government credibility.

As noted development economist Gunnar Myrdal comments, "It is with the people in this elite that all business has to be concluded. Even aid has to be negotiated through them."[2] The effect, says Myrdal, is that "the power of the ruling elite...is then backed up." In part for this reason he concludes that aid from the industrial countries has "undoubtedly strengthened the inegalitarian economic and social power structure in the underdeveloped countries that stands as the main impediment to institutional reforms."

As long as such governments receive outside support in the form of economic and military aid and trade, they can more effectively resist reforms essential to equitable development, rather than inducing positive changes.[3] In Nicaragua, for example, $300 million in U.S. aid to Somoza's narrowly based, oppressive government set the stage for an even more bloody and destructive confrontation. In 1978-1979, Somoza's National Guard, armed principally by the United States, leveled so much of the country in genocidal combat against the overwhelming majority of the Nicaraguan people that decades are needed to rebuild.

In 1980, in El Salvador, we are seeing a tragic repetition. While every report from that country describes the bloody repression, President Carter is trying to increase economic and military aid to the ruling junta. The Carter administration's rationale is that aid is needed to prevent chaos and to carry out the announced land reform. In 1980, however, Amnesty International issued a report accusing the Salvadoran government of using its land reform as a pretext for attacking the peasants, especially those involved in grassroots peasant organizations. While the Salvadoran government claims to have sent troops to the countryside to occupy the plantations it is expropriating, Amnesty International has charged that the troops are brutally murdering peasants and children. In February 1980, Archbishop Oscar A. Romero, El Salvador's leading church figure, widely known as a conservative, pleaded for a withholding of all U.S. aid until reforms were enacted. "The United States should understand the armed forces' position is in favor of the oligarchy. It is brutally repressive and while it does not change, the aid should not be given."[4] Only weeks after this statement, Archbishop Romero was murdered.

The U.S. government clings to regimes that favor U.S. corporate and military interests—no matter how brutally those regimes repress their own people—until they appear on the verge of collapse. Only then, perhaps, is aid suspended in an effort to promote a "moderate" solution that protects the structural status quo.

Ever since the U.S. Marines helped to install the Somoza family in state power in 1933, the Nicaraguan government has been known as one of the world's most notorious human rights violators. Yet in fiscal 1978, the Carter administration tripled what AID calls its "resource flow" to Somoza's Nicaragua. Even after popular armed uprisings began in early 1978, the Carter administration fought to maintain the level of funding for fiscal year 1979, and also sponsored a $32 million Inter-American Development Bank loan.[5]

Only in the fall of 1978, following prolonged strikes of workers and business owners in a near-successful popular insurrection led by the Sandinista National Liberation Front, did President Carter finally suspend aid to Somoza. The suspension merely interrupted the planning of new projects. It allowed all AID project funds "in the pipeline," as well as the 11-member U.S. military advisory group, to continue. As Somoza's prospects for remaining in power dimmed during the liberation struggle which lasted more than one year, Carter administration officials tried in vain to identify an´ alternative group of leaders who could maintain "somozismo" without Somoza.

On whose side?

So far we have discussed the U.S. government's persistent support of repressive regimes. Further evidence that the U.S. government puts its weight against genuine reform can be compiled from a review of recent cases in which the United States has cut off aid just when meaningful structural reforms are under way.

Thailand. From 1973 to 1976, a civilian Thai government allowed peasants to organize for land and other agrarian reforms. The Farmers Federation of Thailand, founded in 1974, united one and one-half million farmers in a movement with great potential strength. Workers' organizations succeeded in doubling the minimum wage. During this period, AID sharply curtailed economic assistance and even prepared to eliminate it. Under the civilian regimes, only U.S. *military* assistance to Thailand grew, expanding threefold.[6]

In 1976, a military coup brought to power a government that brutally repressed workers, peasants, students, and religious groups who had been pressuring for progressive reforms. Many Americans remember the moving television and news magazine coverage of the ruthless police attacks on those resisting the military coup. Few Americans know, however, that the weapons used were supplied under the U.S.-funded Narcotics Control Program.[7] After the military coup, AID's program in Thailand suddenly expanded sevenfold.[8] While visiting Thailand in early 1978, we discovered AID's programs concentrated in the provinces which the military regime has designated "sensitive" due to ongoing resistance.

Chile. Economic aid was denied to the civilian government, elected in 1970, which sought to implement in an electoral and democratic manner the very reforms U.S. aid agencies *talk* about. U.S. aid was immediately restored in 1973, after a military junta overthrew the elected and increasingly popular government. Since that time, the military junta has ruthlessly taken millions of acres of land from peasants and sought to wipe out any dissent against its policies.[9]

Nicaragua today. In early 1980, as the Nicaraguan government began to carry out an ambitious literacy campaign—to re-orient basic social services such as health care toward the needs of the majority and to deliberate on the most just and effective type of agrarian reform—the U.S. Congress debated whether or not to give aid to Nicaragua. After lengthy debate, aid was finally approved by five votes but at this date still hangs in limbo because of a general freeze on new appropriations. At one stage, the legislation included a stipulation that aid would be cut off unless democratic elections were held. In the final version of the bill, the President was instructed to "encourage" elections in Nicaragua.* Few Americans are prepared to ask why Congress agonized over aid to Nicaragua today when aid to Nicaragua was hardly questioned while Somoza was in power. And why does massive aid flow without reservation to autocrats such as Marcos in the Philippines?

Unspoken but understood

The truth is that however abhorrent such regimes are to most Americans, they share common interests with U.S. corporate lobbyists and foreign policy decisionmakers.

Governments in the Philippines, South Korea, Indonesia and similar regimes provide a "favorable climate" for multinational corporate investments which provides few, if any, restrictions on import, export, pricing and profit-repatriation activities. Countries with such governments have become sources of raw materials and low-paid, unorganized labor upon which ever-expanding corporate profits depend. Such regimes also welcome U.S. foreign military installations, partly as a guarantor of their own police states. To refuse to support repressive regimes such as those we have been describing would be to risk supporting democratic economic alternatives. Initiatives such as those in Nicaragua today pose a threat to powerful interests in the United States, both directly in terms of corporate investments and indirectly in terms of a potential example of people actively engaged in redistribution of economic and political power.

---

* Another stipulation on the proposed loan to Nicaragua is that 60 percent of it be earmarked for the private business sector. Nicaraguans, therefore, are not free to decide whether education or health services, for example, might not be a better use of the funds.

4

QUESTION

If more of U.S. development aid were channeled through multilateral lending institutions such as the World Bank, wouldn't that solve the problem of our aid dollars being used for narrow foreign policy and corporate purposes?

RESPONSE International agencies are often seen as neutral since they are supposedly not beholden to any single government. The World Bank† goes to considerable lengths to publicize its "professional" (implying "apolitical") stance. A brief examination of country loan allocations by the World Bank, however, suggests that it is no more impartial to the resource, investment and security interests of multinational corporations and the governments they strongly influence than are the U.S. bilateral programs.

While 75 countries received loans from the World Bank in FY 1979,* a mere 10 of them received over 56 percent of the total. (See Chart III.) Five governments among the 10 top recipients of U.S. bilateral economic aid are also among the 10 top World Bank recipients. They are Egypt, Indonesia, India, the Philippines, and Turkey. Only *two* of the Bank's 10 top loan recipients were countries the Bank classifies as "low income."[1]

The majority of the Bank's leading recipients, governments such as those of Indonesia, Brazil, Mexico, South Korea, the Philippines and Colombia, are notorious for their neglect of policies helpful to the poor. In Africa south of the Sahara, the Bank's most favored country has been Nigeria—one of the higher-income African nations—where substantial revenues from its 1970s oil boom were squandered on the military, elite-oriented education, imports of luxury consumer goods, and prestige building projects of no benefit to the poor.[2]

The World Bank also shows no

---

† See "A Primer: Some Essential Facts about the Aid Establishment" at the end of this book for an in-depth description.

* Throughout, the World Bank refers to both the World Bank (International Bank for Reconstruction and Development, IBRD) together with the International Development Association (IDA), both of which are part of the World Bank Group. See "Primer."

Xavantes hydroelectric power project, Paranapanema River, Brazil, funded by the World Bank.

hesitation about lending to human rights violators; in fact, it appears to reward them. Almost one-quarter of all World Bank loans in FY 1979 were allocated to four governments widely recognized as systematic violators of human rights (Brazil, Indonesia, South Korea and the Philippines).[3] Four countries that have suffered military takeovers or the imposition of martial law since the early 1970s (Uruguay, Chile, the Philippines and Argentina) received a sevenfold increase in World Bank lending by 1979, while other Bank lending increased only threefold.[4]

The Bank, in fact, has a freer hand than do U.S. bilateral aid programs, which are more readily influenced by pressure from U.S. religious and other humanitarian organizations. The Bank can, therefore, provide an alternative channel for economic support to governments when U.S. bilateral channels are blocked. Such has been the case with Chile under General Pinochet and with another widely condemned human rights violator, Brazil. (Brazil is the Bank's third largest loan recipient.[5])

Mobutu's Zaire, formerly the Belgian Congo, exemplifies the type of government that consistently receives World Bank support.[6] After the CIA-promoted murder of the popular Patrice Lumumba in 1961, President Mobutu was installed with U.S. and European covert and military support in 1966. Since then he has been saved twice from popular uprising by U.S.-supported interventions. The World Bank Group† has extended $468 million to the Mobutu government through mid-1979.[7]

Mobutu keeps mineral-rich Zaire wide open for exploitation by multinational corporations. Forty-five percent of the cobalt used in the United States is mined in Zaire. Despite Zaire's enormous mineral wealth, the overwhelming majority of the country's 20 million rural people (90 percent of the total population) are poor and underfed.[8] According to World Bank statistics, the per capita supply of protein in Zaire is among the lowest in the world.[9] The infant mortality rate is conservatively estimated at 160 per 1,000 live births, among the highest in the world.[10]

At the time of independence from Belgium in 1960, Zaire was a food exporter. Now the country spends over $300 million on food imports, including beef, fruits and vegetables from Zimbabwe and South Africa.[11] Fleeing hunger and repression, hundreds of thousands have sought refuge in neighboring countries. In a January 1978 anti-government uprising, 700 to 1,000 villagers in Bandundu—men, women and children—were massacred by the government.[12] Yet a few months later the White House proclaimed the Mobutu regime a "moderate government" and President Carter rushed in U.S. military planes to transport French and Belgian troops to crush a widespread revolt against the Mobutu regime. At about the same time, the World Bank, with U.S. support, awarded the financially strapped regime yet another project loan, this time for the rehabilitation of oil-palm plantations managed by the giant Unilever Corporation and two Belgian multinationals.[13]

The World Bank is not the only multilateral bank. There is also the Asian Development Bank, the African Development Bank, and the Inter-American Development Bank, known as International these countries are the main beneficiaries of IDB loans...the largest amounts are going to the countries with the least poverty.[15]

The multilaterals and human rights

An amendment to the 1977 Foreign Assistance Act instructs the U.S. executive director in each multilateral development bank† to oppose a proposed loan to any country whose government consistently and grossly violates human rights, unless such assistance is "directed specifically to

---

". . . neither the poorest countries nor the poor within these countries are the main beneficiaries of IDB loans. . ."

Financial Institutions (IFIs).† As a group, through 1978, they made loans totaling $59 billion. Only 30 percent of this lending has gone to "low income" countries, an amount virtually equaled by their lending to a handful of "high incomes" and advanced Mediterranean countries such as Greece and "centrally planned" countries such as Yugoslavia.[14]

An independent study of the loan allocation of the Inter-American Development Bank (IDB) found little change in the "target groups" to which it channeled funds between 1972 and 1979. The evaluation concludes, "In summary, neither the poorest countries nor the poor within programs that serve basic needs of the country's citizens." How has this directive, known as the Harkin Amendment, been implemented?

First, in 1978, the President instructed all U.S. executive directors to oppose all loans by the IFIs to Cuba, Angola, Mozambique, Vietnam, Cambodia, Laos and Uganda.[16] This categorical denial of funds is not consistent with the amendment: Is it not as possible that a loan might help meet citizens' basic needs in these countries as in other countries where the United States has approved loans, no matter how human rights situations are judged in each of these countries? (In some of these very countries

CHART III

Ten Top Recipients Get 56 Percent of World Bank (IBRD and IDA) Assistance, FY 1979 ($ millions)—July 1, 1978-June 30, 1979

1. India*	**$1,492.0**
2. Indonesia*	**830.0**
3. Brazil	**674.0**
4. Mexico	**552.0**
5. Korea, Republic of	**397.0**
6. Philippines	**395.5**
7. Morocco	**349.0**
8. Egypt	**322.5**
9. Turkey	**312.5**
10. Colombia	**311.5**
Ten top recipients:	**$5,636.0**
All 65 others:	**4,374.5**
Total Assistance FY 1979:	**$10,010.5**
Portion of assistance to ten top recipients:	56.3 percent

* "low-income" World Bank definition

diverse observers have noted the exceptional success of programs meeting basic needs such as food, health, shelter and education.)

But with regard to many other governments, even some internationally recognized human rights violators, U.S. policymakers seem predisposed to assume that a particular loan would serve the needs of the people. In so doing, they switch to the rationalization that denial would "doubly punish the poor," a view we have just analyzed. Between October 1977 and December 1978, the United States through its executive directors in the IFIs opposed 45 loans to 14 countries on human rights grounds while approving 35 loans *to the very same countries.* The approved loans were said to meet basic needs or were granted because human rights conditions were said to be improving. The U.S. negative votes were meaningless anyway because all the loans to the 14 named human rights violators were ultimately approved.[17]

Sometimes the U.S. voting pattern seems quite arbitrary. In the case of Boukassa's Central African Empire, the U.S. director at the African Development Bank thought a roads project deserved approval on ''basic needs'' grounds, despite acknowledged gross human rights violations. At the same time, the U.S. director at the Inter-American Development Bank voted not to fund roads in rights-violators Chile and Uruguay. Roads for the Chung Hee Park martial law government in South Korea were approved by the U.S. director at the Asian Development Bank. A program for irrigation in the Philippines was awarded by the U.S. director at the Asian Development Bank on basic needs grounds; he was directed to vote against the same type of program for Vietnam.[18]

At other times it is clear that the political interests of the major western powers controlling the World Bank hold sway. To insure congressional passage of new appropriations for the Bank, Robert McNamara promised Vietnam's adversaries in the U.S. Congress that no new loans would be extended to Vietnam during fiscal year 1980. McNamara rationalized his move by declaring that the Vietnamese government was not capable of carrying out development programs. Yet it was clear to all that he was bowing to the interests of those wanting to punish the Vietnamese for their role in overthrowing the Pol Pot regime in neighboring Cambodia. By contrast, neither members of the U.S. Congress nor McNamara ever suggested that a similar cutoff should be applied to Tanzania after it invaded Uganda.

The World Bank does not operate fundamentally differently than U.S. bilateral assistance programs. Its loan decisions, including human rights restrictions, are manipulated to reward or to punish regimes according to narrowly defined policy interests of the U.S. (and other economically dominant governments). By ''narrowly defined'' we mean shaped by the interests of multinational corporations, Cold War rivalry, and hostility to any potentially threatening contrast to the concentrated power structure that has taken hold of the United States.

5

QUESTION

Doesn't U.S. foreign aid go predominantly to agriculture and rural development?

RESPONSE Listening to top policymakers of AID† and the World Bank,† one would certainly think so. In statements to Congress and to the public, they stress that since the early 1970s significantly greater portions of their program funds have been earmarked for agriculture, nutrition and rural development projects.[1]

Appropriate terminology

Rather than a redirection of development programs, we have discovered renamed development programs. With the American public increasingly concerned about hunger and some members of Congress questioning AID critically, AID has been careful to develop an "appropriate terminology." In recent AID presentations to Congress, for instance, an ever-wider range of projects is included under the program heading "Food and Nutrition." Many AID officials boast that over half of the agency's project funds now go for "Food and Nutrition."* What we have discovered is that AID has turned "Food and Nutrition" into a catch-all category to include almost anything it finances outside the boundaries of major urban areas: electrification, roads, agricultural institutions and even "satellite application and training."

Electrification as "Food and Nutrition"

AID now lists electrification projects under the "Food and Nutrition" funding category. Rural electrification projects account for 40 percent of AID's "Food and Nutrition" lending in Asia.[3]

Does rural electrification benefit the poor? According to AID's own studies the rural poor themselves generally rank electrification very low on their list of priorities. One useful report prepared, in fact, for AID, draws upon studies carried out in Central America, Colombia and the Philippines. The author, Judith Tendler, reaches this conclusion: "Impact studies of rural electrification consistently find that the *household users of rural electricity are the better off among the rural population.* This is not surprising, since household electricity usage requires expenditures

---

† See "A Primer: Some Essential Facts about the Aid Establishment" at the end of this book for an in-depth description.

* It should be noted that "project funds" comprise only about one-quarter of the AID budget. (Three-quarters of the budget is used for the Economic Support Fund,† administrative overhead, and contributions to international organizations.[2])

for hookups, wiring, monthly consumption, and for the purchase of appliances." (emphasis added).[4] Tendler notes that the only way for a rural electric utility to be financially viable may well be by targeting appliance-using customers. Since rural electrification is more costly than urban, ". . . a rural utility will have to promote electricity consumption even more aggressively than the urban utility."[5] If such is the case, "then rural electrification may not be conducive to having its impact directed to the rural poor," concludes Tendler.[6]

Tendler also questions AID's promotion of central system supply as opposed to rural electrification through independent diesel generators. She stresses that central systems require management skills that are scarce in underdeveloped countries and that the impact of inevitable periodic breakdown is greatly magnified in a central system. "Unfortunately," observes Tendler, "the biggest argument against autogeneration [independent diesel units] is that it is easier for AID to finance a big capital project than lots of little ones."[7]

Because of the evidence that household electrification schemes fail to help the poor, Tendler suggests that priority might be given to nonhousehold uses; i.e., rural light industries, but she doubts that AID should subsidize it. She notes that employment-generating effects may not be what they are often assumed to be and that the return to the entrepreneur is so great that no subsidies are needed to induce such use of electricity. Our own interviews with AID officials in Asia give substance to these doubts. Rather than providing jobs to the poor, rural electrification appears to be threatening jobs.

Indonesia. One $36 million project that draws on funds earmarked for "Food and Nutrition" is Rural Electrification I. The U.S. Congress is told that "all" of the two million people in the area will benefit from "increased economic activity."[8] This claim strongly contrasts with the assessment made by the chief of the AID agricultural office in Indonesia when we interviewed him about the likely impact. He predicted that the better-off landholders and shopowners would use the electricity to mill rice mechanically. When asked about the impact it would have on the millions of landless laborers, especially women, who depend on milling work for survival income, he stated that the project's net impact would be fewer jobs for the poor.[9] (The conversion from the hand pounding to mechanical hulling of rice is already well under way on the island of Java. According to the *Wall Street Journal,* new techniques have already eliminated 133 million work days and $50 million in income per year for the landless women of the island.[10])

Without jobs, people go hungry. Electrification categorized as "Food and Nutrition" may be cruel irony indeed.

Water pumps on canals in Chalna, Bangladesh.

Who are the beneficiaries of rural electrification in Indonesia? One clue is that AID has suggested to the state power authority that it use monies in the house-wiring fund, once rolled over, to finance consumer purchases of electric appliances.[11] The same multinational corporations that collaborate with aid institutions to develop electric power also manufacture electric appliances.[12]

Bangladesh. AID is lending $50 million to Bangladesh for rural electrification. This makes rural electrification its second largest program in the country. One of its main uses will be to power irrigation pumps. Who will benefit? Those who own pumps. Who owns the pumps? A small, already better-off group of farmers. The pumps will increase their income, making it possible, indeed probable, that they will expand their holdings and mechanize to the detriment of the small landholders and landless job seekers.

Moreover, as in Indonesia, rural electricity will rapidly lead to the displacement of the hand milling of rice by centralized power-operated mills. At present, 80 percent of all rice produced in Bangladesh is processed in a way that provides about 50 days employment for every rural woman between the ages of 10 and 49, according to a study by the Bangladeshi government.[13] The same study reveals that most of those so employed are in families in the bottom socio-economic third of the rural population.

AID's own evaluations of rural electrification schemes in Costa Rica and Colombia reveal a clear pattern: benefits accrue to the already better-off who are owners of land, mills and dairy operations, not to the poor.[14]

The AID rationale for such large lending for electrification in Bangladesh and other countries—and for the use of such a large part of the local "counterpart" funds†—is that electrification will stimulate the development of rural industries.[15] It is presumed in project plans that textile and food processing plants will be built and provide jobs for the rural poor, 40 percent of whom are now jobless. Since these plants, however, could not compete with other Asian-based factories in the production of export goods and since most of the people in the countryside are too poor even to buy adequate food, who will constitute a profitable market for consumer goods the plants would produce? Rural industry cannot prosper when the distribution of wealth and, therefore, income is skewed as it is in Bangladesh, Indonesia, and Pakistan where AID is pushing ahead with sizable new rural electrification projects. Only with reasonably equitable participation in the economy—primarily made possible through a genuine sharing of control over agricultural resources—can rural electrification serve to build rural industries integrated into the rhythms of agricultural work and oriented toward improved agricultural equipment as well as basic consumer goods for rural people.

In our experience, AID officials, when questioned, concede that a focus on rural electrification as a way to help the poor and hungry is illogical. They then grasp for straws that might justify their huge commitment of funds. One frustrated AID official proffered that rural electrification in Bangladesh would provide the amenities which could "induce government bureaucrats to go out into the countryside."[16]

Rural roads

AID's "Food and Nutrition" category also covers road projects. Here are just a few road projects AID classifies under "Food and Nutrition":

• Pakistan, "Rural Roads Phase II." $100 million in "Food and Nutrition" funds. The project will build or rehabilitate 1,600 miles of roads. The construction cost per mile is $62,500, a sure signal that construction is big on machinery and short on jobs. Each advisor will cost $7,500 per month. AID notes that its longer-term plan is to assist in constructing or rehabilitating a total of 120,000 miles of rural roads in Pakistan. Based on the cost of its present program, this would mean over $7 billion of AID "Food and Nutrition" funds going to roads in Pakistan! AID describes the beneficiaries of this roads project: "Rural families of all income strata will benefit from the project, but the selection criteria for the roads will ensure that the majority of the beneficiaries will be low-income farmers and the rural poor."[17]

• Haiti, "Road Maintenance II." $8.6 million in "Food and Nutrition" funds "to expand and strengthen the Government of Haiti's National Highway Maintenance Service."[18]

• Liberia, "Rural Roads Phase III." $5.2 million in "Food and Nutrition" funds.[19] According to two investigators from the University of Washington, this new interregional highway "will make it more convenient for Firestone (a massive rubber plantation operator) vehicles to traverse the country, but its relationship to the small farmers' economic and social benefits, the avowed goal, is non-existent."[20]

• Bangladesh. Rural roads will cost an incredible $133,000 per mile, roughly 10 times more than the lowest cost rural roads project in comparable countries. Again, it is a "Food and Nutrition" project.[21]

Building rural roads certainly sounds neutral, even beneficial. Yet we have come to understand in country after country that new roads in the context of sharp rural inequalities and a repressive government can harm the poor. Those who benefit most from rural roads are the larger commercial growers for whom better roads help in getting their crops to the cities and ports more efficiently. The middleman who buys from the poor and is fortunate enough to own some kind of truck can also make his operation more lucrative with the help of better roads. (In most rural areas the middleman already profits more on each unit than the peasant who produces the crop.) Moreover, in countries such as the Philippines, Zaire, Thailand and Guatemala where dictatorships attempt to quell rural resistance, rural roads make it easier to move troops and maintain control. Rural roads also open the countryside to those selling factory-made consumer items and processed foods, especially bottled soft drinks and beer. A boom in such novelties can destroy the market for more nutritious local food as well as the livelihood of village craftspeople.* Finally, in countries controlled in the interests of a few, roads can facilitate the exploitation of an area's natural resources—not for the benefit of the local inhabitants, but for local elites and foreign corporate interests.

A colleague who has lived and worked for several years in rural Bangladesh shared with us her view of why the rural transportation system is heavily used now and why paved roads could even hurt the poor that they are supposed to be helping:

Somebody produces rice and straight after harvest he has to sell it because he's in debt. So he sells it to an intinerant merchant. The merchant picks up a very small quantity here and there, and takes it to where it's stored. Two or three months later, when the first guy gets very hungry he buys it back again at a

much higher price than he sold it. He gets into debt again. And after the next harvest he pays off his debt with some of the next crop. So, there's this tremendous merry-go-round of food traveling in circles all over the country.

If you were able to liberate the transport from this unnecessary moving of food, there would be a tremendous amount of transport which could be used for almost anything....

I can only see paved roads benefiting the larger merchants. These roads enable larger merchant operations to move into previously untapped areas....The only major reason I can see for roads is in the hill areas where they are built for military purposes.[22]

Other "Food and Nutrition" projects

Here are two more examples of what we found in AID's 1979 presentation to Congress under the "Food and Nutrition" heading:

• Cameroon, "Satellite Application and Training." $650,000 of "Food and Nutrition" funds. One satellite specialist costs $90,000 per year. Similar satellite projects, all catalogued as "Food and Nutrition," are being promoted by AID around the world. In countries where the majority of the rural population is excluded from ownership of agricultural resources and with world commerce dominated by multinational corporations, it is not the rural majority who will benefit from "a more accurate knowledge of the natural resource base."[23]

• The Philippines. A new $10.3 million "Food and Nutrition" project is called a "Fund for Local Government." Given the internationally infamous level of corruption in the Philippines martial law regime, financing local government hardly seems to be a direct way to help the poor.[24]

Another "appropriate term" to flash in aid circles is "women." The AID presentation

for these relatively elaborate facilities, as well as for foreign consultants' salaries and the education in the United States of scientists and technicians who will work in them.

But, as we document with numerous country studies in our book *Food First: Beyond the Myth of Scarcity*, what the poor majority lacks is not technical research and know-how but economic and political power. It is the lack of power and not a lack of technical know-how that is at the root of their increasing landlessness and exploitation by money-lenders, landlords, mer-

---

... benefits accrue to the already better-off who are owners of land, mills and dairy operations, not to the poor.

---

on this project also names women as beneficiaries of the Philippine local government project since "many women are in positions of authority (including governor) at the local and regional level."

Whose institutions?

"Institutional development" is another type of program activity under AID's "Food and Nutrition" catch-all. In many countries, AID has committed millions of dollars to research institutions in plant sciences, nutrition, health care, family planning and other specializations. Usually AID loans are given to cover costs of construction and equipment

chants and multinational agribusiness. Without an increase in the power of the poor, no amount of technical sophistication on the part of their compatriots will benefit them. Agricultural research will continue to be heavily biased toward the better-off farmers' possibilities (land, irrigation and purchases of fertilizers, machines and pesticides) and needs (cash cropping and diminished dependence on hired labor). In such countries, exceptional, well-intentioned researchers who have attempted to counter those biases have often found themselves deported and even physically attacked.

When new technical research benefits the better-off, we must never forget their further enrichment comes *at the expense of* the poor. Only with the prior redistribution of power over productive resources is it possible for technical research to serve the interests of the majority.[25]

While writing this book, we met two people whose experiences embodied this lesson. In Nicaragua, in October 1979, we met two French agronomists who had been sent there several years earlier with other French agronomists as part of their government's aid program. After several months of work in Somoza's Nicaragua they resigned, stating that current power realities in the countryside made their work serve only the enemies of the poor. The two later joined the Sandinista National Liberation Front.

Following Nicaragua's liberation in July 1979, they began to put their technical abilities to work with the new government in the countryside. When we told them that we would like to tell others about them, they said we should not say that they are simply applying the science they brought from France. "We are using just as much what we learned from the perceptions and capabilities of the *campesinos* while living and fighting in the countryside as Sandinistas."

"Basic needs" à la the World Bank

World Bank spokespeople parade out figures to demonstrate

Robert McNamara, president of the World Bank Group, at the construction site of the Tarbela Dam, Pakistan.

that more and more of the Bank's lending goes to "basic needs"-type projects. They boast, for example, that "Agriculture and Rural Development" now comprises a significant portion of total lending—one-third in FY 1978, and one-quarter in FY 1979.[26] They trumpet that lending in such areas as nutrition, population planning, education, and water supply has grown in order to provide more "services" to the poor.

Yet our investigations reveal a pattern very similar to what we found with AID's programs: even the loans characterized as "meeting the basic needs of the poor" go overwhelmingly to build infrastructure—roads, irrigation, electrification, research facilities, fancy foreign-designed buildings, and the like. Credit for agriculture, the program promoted as most directly targeting small farmers, has received cumulatively less than three percent of World Bank lending. (Our response to Question 7 doubts whether even that reaches or helps many small farmers.)

In 1976, an external advisory panel reviewed the World Bank's policies and programs. The report was critical of the Bank in several areas. It noted that of the 11 population projects reviewed, three-quarters of the project budgets went for hardware (buildings, equipment and vehicles) and that only a small fraction of the hardware use related to family planning. The report also noted that the officials in recipient countries had resented the "heavy-handed" pressure tactics used by the Bank to get them to accept the projects "as conceived and planned by the World Bank."[27]

Indonesia. At least 50 percent of a World Bank nutrition project went for "bricks and mortar"—motor vehicles and fancy equipment for fancy buildings—one American working with the United Nations in Indonesia told us. He found it almost impossible to convince Bank officials that one small-scale village pilot project was essential to meet project goals.[28]

Niger. The World Bank is supplying 90 percent of the Maradi Rural Development Project's 1975 budget of almost $12 million. Funds for buildings, civil works, roads, vehicles and maintenance comprise 36 percent of the project baseline costs. The largest single expenditure is for staff salaries, with almost $1 million going to expatriate staff.

Total agricultural credit offered to farmers will be less than $1 million.[29]

Brazil. The Bank is financing one-third of the Bahia Rural Development Project in Paraguacu, which began in 1978. Over one-fifth of the project expenditures will be for roads. The fact that one-third of the road costs will be in foreign exchange—covered by Bank lending—is evidence that the roads will be built with few local resources.[30] The Paraiba Rural Development Project in

Brejo is similar: roads alone will consume one-quarter of the total project costs. Again, one-third of the road costs are in the form of foreign exchange lent by the Bank.[31]

Thailand. The World Bank will provide financing for part of a $56 million agricultural extension project. Almost 40 percent of the Bank loan of $28 million will finance vehicles, equipment and furniture, including mobile audio-visual units. Over $1 million is to be spent on largely imported, sophisticated audio-visual equipment.[32]

Mexico. According to the Bank's appraisal report of the giant $295 million Pider Rural Development Project, more funds (36 percent) will be spent on "infrastructure" than for credit to the farmers supposedly helped by the program.[33]

We are not against roads or other infrastructure. What we are saying is that such projects leave untouched the structure of control that generates needless deprivation. Still worse, such projects most often benefit those already in power, reinforcing the stranglehold of a relative few over productive assets, a stranglehold that generates poverty and thwarts food security.

When we investigated the Bank-funded Rural Development I project in Bangladesh, for example, we learned that rural works projects designed to maximize local labor input had been diverted from local rural works committees by rich contractors. These contractors, using capital-intensive methods, built roads and markets quickly and shoddily —but quite lucratively for them. World Bank internal reports disclosed that recently completed marketplaces were in "deplorable condition" and that the newly built roads were already partially washed away.[34] It is clear who the winners are. The losers are the rural poor. It is they who must ultimately pay for the contractors' "services" by producing cash crops for export to earn foreign exchange.

The Bank's public service projects, such as water or sewage projects for urban slums, provide a further example of the Bank's blindness to the economic realities in which they must operate. In Indonesia, a *Wall Street Journal* investigator found that the Bank's urban water and sewage projects resulted immediately in higher market values for all of the dwellings in the slum area.[35] Property taxes began to increase at the rate of 15 percent a year. The result? The poor—the supposed beneficiaries of the new services—had to sell to better-off people and move to illegal squatter settlements on Jakarta's outskirts. Similar results have occurred in Bank "urban development" projects in the Philippines, Brazil and elsewhere.[36]

Urban magnet

Current development literature devotes considerable attention to

Rice planting, the Philippines.

the problem of "rural-urban migration"; i.e., the problem of more and more of the impoverished people in rural areas moving to urban areas in desperate search for employment. Many rural development projects are partially rationalized with the claim that they help to stem the tide of this rural outmigration. The irony is that AID and World Bank projects typically draw people *out* of rural areas into the cities, according to a 1979 survey conducted for AID. The report explains the apparent irony: such migration to the cities is due in large part to the fact that "operating and project expenditures for (aid) agency rural-oriented activities are made primarily in the capital cities."[37] The report goes on: "Employment generated by these expenditures and their multipliers provide a significant incentive for rural-urban migration." Of course, few who flee landlessness and joblessness in the countryside find satisfactory work in the cities. Most end up in wretched slums, refugees from both the countryside and the city.

6

If only one-quarter of World Bank loans are used for agriculture and rural development, what does the World Bank do with the rest?

RESPONSE Billions of dollars are lent annually for highways, industrial and power projects, mining, port facilities, tourism and other infrastructural projects.[1] Policymakers attempt to rationalize these program priorities by using a modified version of the widely discredited "trickle-down" theory—the notion that overall economic growth eventually benefits the poor majority. World Bank† president Robert McNamara articulates its latest rendition in an interview with the *New York Times*: "...the Bank's investment program is designed to expand production....It has two components. The first consists of projects designed to strengthen the economies in general—for example power plants, roads, irrigation works, fertilizer plants. The second component consists of projects directed or projects aimed directly at increasing the productivity of the rural and urban poor."[2]

In the view of policymakers like Robert McNamara, "strengthening the economies in general" is neutral: while the approach may not selectively help the poor, at least it doesn't hurt them. Overlooked in such a view is what most people with a commonsense understanding of development grasp: no development is neutral; the expansion of one sector is almost always at the expense of another. In other words, when some gain, others lose.

The neatly separated sectors of the economy found in a typical aid agency report fail to reflect the reality of an interconnected economic system within recipient countries. For example, World Bank and other multilateral lending† to finance power development in urban areas has wreaked havoc on the lives of rural poor. In northeast Brazil, the Bank is financing part of a $400 million hydroelectric power and irrigation scheme. A 200-mile stretch along the São Francisco River has been flooded, uprooting 70,000 people (mostly small farm families) from their homes and livelihoods.[3] According to local church officials they have not been adequately compensated for their losses nor provided with decent alternatives. The area's

---

† See "A Primer: Some Essential Facts about the Aid Establishment" at the end of this book for an in-depth description.

Catholic bishop reports that because food must now be imported into the area, shortages and higher prices are worsening the already high degree of malnutrition.[4] Electricity from the dam will be transmitted to the coastal cities. Irrigation waters will serve large-scale, mechanized farms, financed by the Inter-American Development Bank, and geared to export markets.[5]

Along the Chico River in the Philippines, the Bank has promoted the development of a four-dam hydro-power project costing over $1 billion. In order to complete what will be Asia's largest hydro-power project, more than 10,000 Kalingan farmers will be forced to abandon their native homes and fields. Manila officials have employed divisive tactics which pit tribe against tribe to weaken their resistance. They have even supplied weapons to those tribal leaders who will support the project. Thus, armed opposition to the project's implementation has grown among the local people. The 60th Philippine Constabulary Battalion has been called into the project area to quell continued protests.[6]

Similarly, we fear for those who happened to live in the path of a reservoir created by the Tarbela Dam project in Pakistan. The final World Bank report on the completion of the project

Tarbela Dam, Indus River, Pakistan. International funding for the project is administered by the World Bank.

notes: "Filling [of the reservoir] began on schedule, and initially went according to plan except that for a short period the rise of the reservoir had to be slowed to allow some of the 80,000 people who had been slow to move out of the reservoir area to get away from the rising waters."[7]

These are examples of the physical displacement and the heightened deprivation of the poor directly related to Bank-financed infrastructural projects. But the primary impact of such investments on the poor majority is less directly measurable. The billions of dollars invested in resorts, port facilities, highways and industrial parks are all votes for the continuation of an export-oriented economy geared to the needs and tastes of a few elite and foreign consumers. To those relative few now benefiting from the status quo, such World Bank loans provide strong incentives to resist all change. World Bank lending is, therefore, a formidable block in the path of fundamental reorganization of power and priorities, a prerequisite to the self reliance of the poor.

More than a lender

The World Bank may get appropriations from congresses and parliaments by focusing attention on agriculture and rural development. But it also makes it its business to shape the overall economic and, therefore, social plans of the countries to which it lends.[8] In this role, too, the Bank has a powerful impact on the poor.

In many countries the Bank's "country economic reports" become the guidelines for a national development plan. In an increasing number of countries the Bank assembles and chairs a consortium of the principal bilateral and multilateral lenders in order to "coordinate" the flow of aid. By 1979, the Bank had established permanent missions in 18 underdeveloped countries, often physically located within the offices of national planning ministries and central banks. In some countries, including Bangladesh, the Bank is quietly placing and lending funds for advisors to key ministries of the government.

The Bank, together with its partner the International Monetary Fund (IMF)†, forms teams of international auditors to evaluate the fiscal policies of countries and to formulate changes. These changes are tantamount to conditions for borrowing. The Bank's trump card is that it establishes for each country an international credit rating that determines how much a government is likely to be able to borrow from both public and private sources.

The World Bank's influence over development strategies, therefore, cannot be taken lightly. As the Bank itself notes: "IDA's [part of the World Bank Group] borrowers, in particular, would be unlikely to obtain financing on terms as satisfactory as IDA's from any other source. They are therefore unlikely to disregard the kind of advice they may be given by the Bank IDA missions....'"[9] Not surprisingly, the Bank is increasingly spoken of as *the* power in many of the third world countries in which we have carried out field research.

An article in the British *Guardian* gives some notion of how that power can be used in a country like Bangladesh:

> ...devaluation is only the most dramatic measure in the World Bank programme, which to be successful must be accompanied by fiscal and other changes which will restore monetary stability. An integral part of the programme is the creation of a "favourable investment climate".... In spite of the clinically neutral language...the stabilization programme is not simply a technical exercise in monetary management. It amounts to imposing lower real incomes mainly on the urban and other working classes.[10]

Similarly, in Indonesia the World Bank chairs a consortium of all the government's creditors, including bilateral lenders, multinational development banks and the International Monetary Fund. In its role as coordinator of all lenders as well as major lender itself (Indonesia is the second largest recipient of World Bank loans), the World Bank holds decisive power over Indonesia's economy.

In 1979, the World Bank mapped a new development strategy for Indonesia that places the greatest stress on "export-oriented industrialization." The Bank's recommendations disregard the fact that the livelihood of most Indonesians comes from working the land. Agriculture is overlooked. Instead, the Bank proclaims that "the single most important overall policy requirement...is to get the industrial sector going on a sound basis with as little protection as possible and with considerable export orientation...."[11] The Bank favors "export-processing zones" with special incentives for foreign investors, including inducements to set up shop near congested Jakarta and in east and central Java. The Bank promotes the "opportunity" for investors provided by Indonesia's poor—the "largest remaining pool of inexpensive and relatively literate labor in East Asia." The wages for unskilled labor are "among the lowest in the world," notes the Bank. To further entice corporate investors the Bank stresses that "labor is not unionized and the government has largely refrained from intervening in the labor market...."[12]

In addition to questioning the value of development whose major goal is to link foreign export-oriented firms to underpaid and powerless workers, we also question the economics of the Bank's "new" strategy for Indonesia. For instance, how many jobs will actually be created? The *Wall Street Journal* comments:

> In many nations beset by widespread poverty, invest-

ment and trade by multinationals has done little to create jobs. There is even evidence that foreign investment, along with unenlightened government policies, has done just the opposite: make jobs disappear . . . .

. . . the planning agency has discovered that exports, which have multiplied eightfold with the aid of foreign oil and mineral companies, support 60,000 *fewer* jobs today than they did back in 1971. (emphasis added)[13]

While the Bank would focus public attention on its projects designated to meet "basic needs," it is in its less visible role as overall molder of economic policy that the Bank has its most powerful impact on the lives of the millions of poor.

Worker in rice fields, Casamance region, Senegal.

7

Don't U.S. AID-funded and World Bank-funded agriculture and rural development projects now concentrate on small farmers?

RESPONSE The World Bank† has allocated cumulatively about 13 percent of its "agriculture and rural development funds" to agricultural credit.¹ In 1975, the Bank stated that almost half of such funds over the next five years would go to small farmers.² This sounds commendable until one stops to consider that this means that more than half of rural credit goes to medium and large farmers who at most constitute only 20 percent of all third world landholders.³ Moreover, the point we have repeated throughout this book should not be forgotten here: credit or any other support for those in control of the rural power structure does not merely *bypass* the poor majority; it threatens them by aiding their adversaries.

In addition, we must question those credit programs supposedly designated for the "small farmer."

Whether or not a lending agency's project, such as a credit and agricultural extension scheme, reaches small farmers depends in part on how the agency defines "small." What might sound like a small farmer to a North American may well include much of the landed elite in many third world countries.

Criteria for credit

In 1977, the U.S. Comptroller General's office examined a number of AID-financed "small farmer" credit schemes in Latin America and the Caribbean. It found the eligibility criteria for loans to be so broad that they include "many medium and large farmers."⁴

An AID loan in Panama to build cooperative credit groups defines a small farmer as one owning 50 acres or less and having assets of less than $15,000. But over half of the farmers in Panama work 12 acres or less.⁵

Often such credit projects specify a limit on the size of a loan in order to make, theoretically, the credit more available to small landholders. But even when the lending agency sets the ceiling low enough not to attract the rural elite and within reach of poor landholders, recipient governments allied with large landhold-

---

† See "A Primer: Some Essential Facts about the Aid Establishment" at the end of this book for an in-depth description.

ers can simply ignore the guidelines. In Somoza's Nicaragua, a loan limit was set at $120 according to AID's program guideline. An AID-funded evaluation of the program, however, showed that the government had pushed the loan limit to $590, five times the annual income of 70 percent of the rural people in Nicaragua.[6] Clearly, the majority could not qualify for a loan of such magnitude.

Credit schemes can also specify a minimum number of acres a farmer must have to be eligible for a new loan. An AID "new directions"† rural credit project in a Central American country, designed to help the rural poor, set the minimum land holding so high that it excluded two-thirds of the farmers in five communities studied by anthropologist Peggy Barlett from Emory University. Dr. Barlett warned AID that the project in practice "is aimed at the upper middle stratum of the rural areas" and "if successful, the project can be expected to increase the gap between this rural elite and the poor majority." She also noted that 55 percent of the $5.5 million loan goes to "middle-class Costa Ricans who administer and carry out the programs, to education institutions in Costa Rica and elsewhere, and to contractors." The AID response to this critical appraisal was that the project was already under way and, therefore, could not be changed.[7]

In other instances, AID has openly acknowledged that its loan programs are going to the large landholders. Its program in Bolivia is one case in point. But rather than admitting the contradiction with its "small farm" rhetoric, AID simply explains that it is "this target group [that] could most effectively use production credit."[8]

In earlier writing, we at the Institute for Food and Development Policy made a similar critique of World Bank "small farmer" credit programs—that they do not reach the small farmers. The Bank responded in an internal memorandum, saying that such criticism is out of date because the Bank has substantially altered its lending criteria in recent years to favor poor farmers. To prove their point the memo cites a 1977 rural credit loan: "A 1977 rural credit loan in the Philippines, the country mentioned here by the Institute, emphasized an increasing share of credit for small borrowers, with 30.6 percent of the funds being loaned to owners of less than 17 acres of land, or less than five fishponds or not more than one fishing vessel or people satisfying some similar criteria."[9] Perhaps 17 acres sounds small to Bank officials in Washington. It is *not* small, however, for those familiar with the rural Philippines. Consulting the most recent survey of third world land tenure, conducted by Cornell University, we find that the Bank's low-end criteria (and even then for only 30.6 percent of total loans!) is about double the size of the average farm in the Philippines.[10] Moreover, as the Cornell study emphasizes, the vast major-

Masai district, Kenya. Livestock development programs funded by the International Development Association of the World Bank.

ity of rural Filipinos are "landless or nearlandless" and can survive only by selling their labor and that of their families to large landholders.

A large World Bank-financed livestock project in Kenya allocates loan credits in the following manner: 54 percent for a few commercial ranchers; 33 percent for a few company ranches; nine percent for 42 individual ranches; and four percent for 25 group ranches supporting 1,500 ranchers. Bank economist Uma Lele notes that even the "employment potential is low." She also gives a classic Bank rationalization for so much money benefiting so few. "The tax revenues generated from these ranches are expected to help the government provide rural services to other needy areas."[11] The "trickle-down"

theory is apparently still believed at the Bank.

A livestock project in Honduras which was investigated by a House appropriations subcommittee has received three successive loans totally $23.2 million from the International Development Agency (IDA),† the soft-loan arm of the World Bank that supposedly directs its projects specifically toward the poor. Subcommittee investigators analyzed the records of loan recipients and found that the average size of loans for all three projects ranged from $25,000 to $59,000 and that the vast majority of the farmers receiving credit from the projects owned more than 150 hectares (375 acres) of land. As the investigators reported, "The subborrowers visited were relatively prosperous ranchers with well-managed farms who had increased beef or dairy production markedly through the loans under the project...."[12] The subcommittee noted by contrast: "Of the rural poor in the country, 60 percent have per capita income less than $100, of which half are less than $60. Local officials point out that they have been unable to devise any program to reach such people and that instant projects were not designed for and cannot reach the rural poor who are landless or existing on one or two hectares."[13]

How do agencies produce so many "poor beneficiaries," used when touting their projects before the public? It is quite simple. They often count *everyone* living in a "project area." [14] The rationale is that both large and small farmers can profit from modern farming inputs in pro-portion to their land ownership. And the landless? The theory goes that they will have more work since the farming inputs generate greater production.

"Going to the big boys"

Project planning documents of AID and the World Bank read like abstract exercises in economics, divorced from political, social and cultural factors. On the rare occasion that conflicts of interest are even acknowledged, the implications for the implementation of a project are overlooked. Government and other actors are all presumed to be working together to alleviate poverty. They assume that rural poor people can be "reached" from the top down through government programs. The real world, unfortunately, is quite different.

Tubewell in Bangladesh funded in part by the International Development Association of the World Bank.

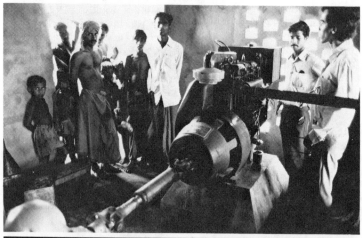

To better understand how a project purportedly designed to selectively reach the small farmer ends up enriching the better-off at the expense of the poor, let's examine an actual case in some detail.

The World Bank provided credit to the government of Bangladesh to fund 3,000 deep tubewells. (A tubewell is a mechanically drilled well, using a pump to bring water to the surface. A tubewell makes possible an extra crop of rice during the dry winter season in northwestern Bangladesh.) According to a Bank press release, each well would serve 25 to 50 small farmers, joined together in a cooperative irrigation group.[15]

Independent researchers and Institute fellows Betsy Hartmann and James Boyce, who lived for nine months in one of the villages covered by the project, learned what was no secret to anyone in the village: the tubewell has become the property of one man, the richest landlord in the village.[16] The touted "cooperative irrigation group" amounts to a few signatures he collected on a scrap of paper. The foreign donors and the Bangladesh government paid $12,000 for each well. This particular landlord paid less than $300 for his well, and much of that was used to bribe local officials. The landlord *will* allow small farmers tilling adjacent plots to use "his" water but he charges an hourly rate so high that few are able to pay. Since the amount of land owned by the rich landowner is only half the area that the tubewell is capable of irrigating, the tubewell will be greatly underutilized. (It is, in fact, this prevalent tubewell underutilization that most irks World Bank technocrats.)

Was the Hartmann and Boyce experience atypical? Apparently, not at all. They expressed their shock to a foreign expert working on the Bank project. He told them:

I no longer ask who is getting the well. I know what the answer will be and I don't want to hear it. One hundred percent of these wells are going to the "big boys." First priority goes to those with the most power and influence: the judges, the magistrates, the members of parliament, the union chairmen. If any tubewells are left over, the local authorities auction them off. The big landlords compete and whoever offers

World Bank "small farmer" credit programs. . .do not reach the small farmers.

the biggest bribe gets the tubewell.[17]

Should the Bank have known this in advance? Are we just proving that hindsight is often clearer than foresight? Not at all. An evaluation carried out for the Swedish International Development Authority (SIDA), an agency that joined the Bank in financing the tubewell project, examined 270 tubewells and concluded:

It is not surprising that the tubewells have been situated on the land of the well-to-do farmers, or that it is the same well-to-do farmers who are the chairmen and managers of the irrigations groups. *It [would have] been more surprising if the tubewells had not been located on their land,* with the existing rural power structure, maintained largely because of the unequal distribution of the land. (emphasis added)[18]

The Bank has nonetheless told the world that the tubewell project is a success. The foreign expert who confided to Hartmann and Boyce that the wells would only go to the "big boys" also commented: "On paper it all sounds quite nice. Here are the peasants organizing to avail themselves of this wonderful resource. When the officials fly in from Washington for a three-day visit to Dacca, they look at these papers. They don't know what is happening out here in the field, and no one is going to tell them."[19]

AID, the World Bank, and the Asian Development Bank have been promoting "integrated rural development" cooperatives in a number of Asian countries. A SIDA study that evaluated the real-world functioning of such cooperatives concluded:

... we are forced to draw the conclusion that the cooperatives have failed, and are likely to continue to fail, to serve as effective instruments in the struggle against poverty, landlessness, inequality and unemployment.

The cooperatives, these "closed clubs of kulaks," as the Planning Commission has labeled them, today work almost exclusively for the benefit of a small minority of the peasantry and, certainly, in favor of some urban-based interests as well. *Landless or nearlandless, the majority of the population, are not participating at all.* (emphasis added)[20]

The SIDA report cited earlier concurs: "Democratically functioning cooperatives never work if land holdings continue to be as unevenly distributed as they are today. To try to keep the big landowners outside the cooperatives . . . is nothing but wishful thinking."[21]

Not neighbors but rivals

What, then, is the real tragedy that results from such projects? That tens of millions of dollars (in reality loans that must be repaid largely by the work of the rural people of Bangladesh) have been wasted? That a resource has been grossly underutilized? That poor farmers have not been helped? Yes, all of these things, but much more.

The Bank's impact should not be understood as simply a failure to help the "target" group. Such a project actually *undercuts* those it is supposed to help by enriching their economic enemies. In the villages studied by Hartmann and Boyce, the large landowner—like his counterparts in other villages —is reported "already to have an eye on the plots nearest his tubewell."[22] Thanks to his new income from the World Bank tubewell, he will be better positioned to buy out the smaller farmers when hard times befall them, thus driving them into the growing ranks of the landless.

One U.N. Food and Agriculture Organization agronomist with 15 years experience in Bangladesh told us, "The thing to remember about the villages is that the people are not neighbors but rivals."[23] Similarly, an anthropologist working with a team studying a disparate group of Bangladesh villages told us that the fundamental social reality is a struggle over land. The well-off do everything possible to get their smaller neighbors indebted to them in order to foreclose on their land; the poor families do everything possible to hold on to the little land that they have. The well-off landowners do not want the small farmers or landless laborers to prosper; they want them to become more *dependent*,

Maijpara, Bangladesh.

more indebted to them.[24]

The rural elite who usurp the tubewell—or the new machine, or the extension workers' guidance, or whatever the Bank projects supposedly earmark for small farmers—will do their best to make sure that their poorer neighbors do not benefit. This is true even if it means vastly underutilizing the new input. Ignoring this constant economic warfare, AID and World Bank projects not only fail in narrow production terms (production in "Rural Development I" villages in Bangladesh, for example, is no higher than elsewhere[25]) but also strengthen the oppressors of the already desperate small farmers and the landless.

A Bangladeshi social scientist sums it up: "The richer classes have ways of bending things to their own advantage. When the structure remains unchanged, the foreign aid, whether or not it comes with an attached clause that it should be so used as to reach the poor, *helps the ruling classes maintain their power and authority* and this is what has been happening in Bangladesh." (emphasis added)[26]

Promoting "marketable surplus" producers

There is another reason why, despite aid agency talk of helping small farmers, aid projects wind up working with the already better-off producers. Much aid is in the form of loans to a government which in turn lends ("subloans") to project beneficiaries. These subloans are used, for example, to purchase farming inputs. Just as the government will have to repay its loan, so must the recipients of the subloans pay back theirs. Thus there is a built-in dynamic likely to channel the loans to those with the possibility of producing what economists call a "marketable surplus"—something left over to sell—so that money can be earned to repay the loan. Poor, small farmers who grow food so that *they* eat better are not likely to produce enough for a marketable surplus and are even less likely to produce enough to be sold for foreign exchange. But only if farmers can grow to sell, especially for export, can loans to their government be repaid. That is what the banks, especially the multilateral development banks, must ultimately be concerned about.

The World Bank itself notes, "Lending only to those with investment opportunities sufficient to produce a significant marketable surplus is perhaps the best way to reduce the level of default."[27] Those with investment opportunities are hardly the small farmers. It is rough to try to be a bank and savior of poor farmers at the same time!

A principal way to insure a marketable surplus is to offer credits for non-food crops. With crops such as cotton, rubber and coffee, virtually all of the production must go to market; it can't possibly be eaten by the producer. Furthermore, as the World Bank notes, "Delinquencies [in loan repayment] have also been reduced when repayment has been coordinated with the marketing of crops that are centrally processed, for example, tobacco, cotton, cocoa, tea, and coffee."[28]

The crops which have the greatest likelihood of producing a marketable surplus are not necessarily those favored by poor, small farmers. For its transmigration project in Sumatra (Way Abung), Indonesia, the World Bank decided that the new settlers shoud grow rubber trees.[29] But these small farmers resisted, saying:

"I'll make more money growing rice."

"I've never worked with rubber and I don't understand it."

"I want to plant food, not something I can't eat."

"The price of rubber fluctuates too much."

"There is no factory nearby so transportation costs will be too high."

"If I spend time each day tapping rubber, I won't have time for other crops."

As a crop in addition to rice, Way Abung farmers much prefer coconut to rubber. Coconut oil is needed for cooking, husks are burned for fuel, and leaves are used in roofing and making walls. Coconut meat and milk can be consumed. If cash is needed, the market is local and does not require costly transportation.

Rubber prevailed, however.

One reason, we were told, was that the World Bank expert on the scene was a rubber specialist, not a coconut specialist. At last count, only 11 percent of the rubber area had been planted. One confidential Bank review of the project noted that such problems result "when the development strategy overlooks the basic economy of the settlers themselves."[30]

Cane sugar has also become a favorite World Bank crop. Visiting Indonesia, we learned that the Bank is financing (thus far to the tune of $50 million) the rebuilding of sugar mills built by the Dutch colonizers in the 19th century. Local farmers, however, did not want to grow sugar cane, in part because they said they could make twice as much by cultivating rice. According to the *Wall Street Journal,* the sugar mill officials were "forcing the unhappy farmers to grow cane at gunpoint."[31]

In late 1978, in response to a *Los Angeles Times* article by the Institute, the World Bank denied that it had provided any loans for non-food export crops since 1973, the year the Bank marks as the beginning of its focus on small farmers and on the hungry. We do not believe this claim. Even the Bank's annual report, its principal public document, lists $258.5 million for loans for crops such as tea, tobacco, jute and rubber.[32] In addition, it lists loans for food crops such as vegetables, sugar and cashews—all explicitly designated as going for export—amounting to $221 million.

Reviewing World Bank documents one sees evidence of loans for commodities which we all would view as useful additions to the diet, not as nutritionless exports—soybeans, vegetables and meat, for example. These commodities are, in fact, only the latest wave in production geared to the local elite and export markets. Bank-promoted vegetables and meat may sound better than tea and cocoa but they are apt to do little more to improve the nutrition of the local poor people.

Livestock investments, for example, have been highly favored by World Bank loans. Between 1971 and 1977, the World Bank there is already notably unequal control over productive resources, promotion of cash crops and exports strengthens the forces that generate hunger. To weigh the impact, one has to ask:

• Does the decision to focus on cash crops and exports represent a choice involving the rural people themselves?

• Who will benefit from the marketing and from the export earnings?

• If the promotion of cash crops and exports is successful, will tenants and self-provisioning farmers find access to land even more difficult as the powerful ex-

---

. . . only if farmers can grow to sell, especially for export, can loans to their government be repaid.

---

lent an average of $141 million annually for livestock projects around the world, with almost half going to the Latin American region.[33] What these Bank loans primarily support is commercial ranching, serving the local elite and foreign consumers growing taste for meat. The Bank claims to have de-emphasized livestock since 1975, when one-third of all agricultural lending was for livestock projects.[34] In 1978, however, the Bank's largest loan in agriculture and rural development went for livestock development in Mexico.[35]

Cash crops and agricultural exports are not necessarily bad. The problem is that in societies where pand their holdings in order to profit from the new export opportunities?

• Has basic food security (minimally freedom from famine) been established with local production so that trade is a *complement* to locally produced staples rather than being a desperate hinge on which survival depends?

Especially the very poor resist being pushed by "aid" into dependency on the local and international market economy. They know, or strongly sense, that commercial farming means greatly heightened risks (often even exacerbating, through monocultural practices, the natural risks of agriculture). One of these risks,

IDA funds are helping to finance a road building program in Uganda.

as ennumerated by political econ-omist Cheryl Payer in her study "The World Bank and the Small Farmers," is the fluctuation of market prices due to events in other parts of the world.[36]

The critical importance of fluc-tuating world prices was under-lined for us in a World Bank re-view of 18 of its projects in sub-Saharan Africa.[37] It notes that production targets were reached or surpassed in only four of the 18 projects. Moreover, it points out that the only reason the rates of return were satisfactory to the farmers is that world market prices sharply increased for the commodities involved. The re-port does not probe the obvious

question: What happens when prices go down? It notes: "Most [Bank] appraisal reports [of the 18 projects] did not explicitly discuss possible farmer reaction to changing prices. Some seem to have ignored this altogether... other appraisal reports seem to have assumed that economic determinants (like relative prices) would not change adversely during the project implementation."[38]

Another example which high-lights the risks that only the better off can afford to take is AID's project to make "successful com-mercial farmers" out of the small coffee growers of Haiti. At the project launching in 1976, AID claimed that the project would increase the yields and, therefore, the income of one-third of Haiti's five million inhabitants. As we read about this project, several reservations came readily to mind and several more were raised for us by a thoughtful critique of the project plans done by Development Alternatives, Inc., a Washington consulting firm.[39]

The farmers who were to be the focus of the project were not, as AID would have us think, under-productive coffee growers. They were, instead, self-provisioning farmers who happened to have a few coffee trees. Producing yams, corn, and other food crops basic to their own needs consumed most of their time. Whatever time and energy remained went into coffee production and its cash return. AID wanted to reverse this food-cash relationship, making these peasant farmers primarily commercial coffee producers and buyers of the food they had been growing. Instead of digging yams year-round, the self-sufficient farmer-turned-coffee-producer would need cash to buy the food to feed his family. Would that cash be there? Even though coffee export prices might be high at the start of the project because of the natural disasters that hit major coffee producers in other countries, what would keep them high once recovery was underway? When production among the world's main producers returns to normal levels, the International Coffee Agreement will undoubtedly enforce quotas. AID could be setting Haiti up for a soon-to-be over-supplied market, a disaster for small farmers who would, for the first time, be dependent on coffee sales for their food, if AID has its way.

There are still more ways in which the plan is fraught with risks for small farmers. Coffee has traditionally been grown as a shaded understory (grown beneath larger bushes or trees). Part of AID's push to increase coffee yields requires reducing the shade coverage—an extremely difficult step to reverse. Once the coverage is removed, yields jump, but so does the need for fertilizer. A farmer previously self-reliant in his capacity to produce coffee will become "virtually dependent on an agricultural input, fertilizer, the source of which he does not control. If the supply of fertilizer dries up, so will his coffee trees," warns the Development Alternatives evaluation.[40] Even if the farmer can buy fertilizer, how sure can he be that the price he will be paid for his coffee beans will justify his investment?

Not surprisingly, we learned from local observers that the credit for the coffee producers is not going to the small farmers anyway, but only to those who "already have resources and can assure repayment."[41] Some poor farmers were almost robbed through the project's credit scheme. In one area, poor farmers invested some of their savings on the promise that they would receive $10 worth of credit for each dollar they put in. The money was paid and loans were applied for, but the loans didn't come. The farmers finally requested that their funds be returned, only to hear that "they can't be located." It finally took pressure from several expatriate development workers to get the money back from unscrupulous local officials.

Who would really benefit most from the increased productivity if it is achieved in Haiti? Coffee marketing in Haiti is largely controlled by powerful middlemen. More than by the volume of their production, farmers' income is determined by these middleman speculators who determine the prices farmers get. Moreover, the tax on coffee is the biggest source of revenue for the Jean-Claude Duvalier (Baby Doc) dictatorship. The farmers, not the speculators or exporters, carry that tax burden.[42] Small, unorganized coffee producers are heavily taxed to pay for government services that, in an elite-dominated country like Haiti, benefit only the tiny upper strata.

Dr. Payer summarizes the additional risks in aid-funded programs for small farmers: greater commercialization without a corresponding increase in their power in the marketplace; higher prices for output; and increased vulnerability to pests when uniformly genetic stock is used. Many poor farmers might especially fear what happens after the heyday of showcase aid projects —especially when input subsidies and market price guarantees, once aid agency financed, are no longer sustainable by the local government. In the end their fear,

notes Payer, is that they are being urged into a gamble in which a few may win, but the majority are likely to lose all that they have.[43]

Keeping these realities in mind, it is not difficult to understand why "small farmer" credit schemes rarely reach the rural poor but rather, at best, the middle level farmers. They alone have enough land to take risks to become prosperous commercial growers. These new entrepreneurs are, in the words of a 1978 Cornell study, "likely to be assertive profit-maximizers, politically active, determined in protecting their position and uninclined to recognize traditional obligations of patronage toward tenants and laborers."[44] (This reality that the poor are linked to the well-off by bonds of exploitation is very different from the World Bank's superficial notion, expressed in its policy paper on rural development, that "the poor are found living alongside the prosperous."[45])

Under the banner of aid to the "small farmer," aid agencies may well be strengthening the power of a growing block in the countryside—the new commercial growers who are likely to stand firmly with the traditional landed elites against efforts by the poor to organize themselves to defend their own interests and to demand a just redistribution of control over farming assets.

Aid to agribusiness

The "small farmer" rhetoric of AID and of the World Bank would have us believe that they no longer promote agribusiness operations. In reality, both agencies' lending promotes agribusiness, including direct assistance to some of the world's largest corporations.

Conveniently for agribusiness interests, aid agency focus on small farmer productivity, notes Cheryl Payer, has come at a time when many multinational agribusiness companies are shifting from the plantation model of direct ownership of vast tracts of land to one of control over production through contracts with small producers and control over markets. Agribusiness has learned that direct ownership of land ties up large amounts of capital, exposes it to all the risks endemic to farming, raises the spectre of a large, often unionized labor

force, runs the risk of oversupplied markets, and makes a foreign company an especially easy target for political attack and nationalization.

Thus, agribusiness increasingly prefers to be the multinational marketer of crops supplied by smallholders under supervised credit schemes. This arrangement throws much of the risk onto the farmers, each too small to have any effective bargaining position. Moreover, as the aid agencies, notably the World Bank, foster "outgrower" schemes of the same export crops—principally tea, rubber, sugar, oil palm, livestock and export vegetables—in a number of different countries, it is easier for the contracting multinational corporations to play one

Melons for export to Europe from San Lorenzo area, Peru. The World Bank helped to build the port at Paita.

production site off against another.[46]

AID financing has made possible the Latin American Agribusiness Development Corporation (LAAD), a holding company that numbers among its 15 shareholders a Chase Manhattan agribusiness subsidiary, the Bank of America, Borden, Cargill, CPC International (Hellmann's mayonnaise, Skippy peanut butter, Knorr soups, etc.), John Deere, Gerber, Goodyear, Castle and Cooke (Dole), Ralston Purina, and ADELA (itself a multinational investment company whose 240 shareholders are large multinational corporations). AID loans to LAAD total $17 million, at only three to four percent rate of interest.[47]

LAAD is designed primarily to help set up (and generally lend start-up capital to) small agribusiness companies in various Latin American countries. The multinational shareholders benefit not so much from LAAD-earned profits* as from the input and marketing opportunities growing out of LAAD's agribusiness projects. In addition, the agribusiness projects established are pilot projects. In other words, funds largely from AID are used as the risk capital in new lines of agribusiness ventures. If a venture pays off, it can be expanded and even duplicated.

By the end of 1978, LAAD had approved almost $32 million in loans to 106 agribusiness projects in Latin America. These projects included processing and marketing beef, and growing and exporting fresh and frozen vegetables, wood products, seafood, cut flowers, ferns and tropical plants, and other specialty items.

AID hired an outside consulting firm to evaluate LAAD in 1974. Although not unsympathetic to LAAD's purposes, the firm reported that LAAD's presence has not produced additional food for those who need it. "The bulk of the product lines handled are either destined for upper middle, upper class consumption, or for export," stated the evaluation.[49] Small farmers and small businessmen had not been helped either. "LAAD's efforts have not, for the most part, been diluted by social motives to reach the small man." Instead, according to the report, LAAD has been "supporting businessmen whose success is predictable."

We fundamentally question whether an aid agency can help the poor by assisting corporations that must seek profitable markets. The poor are obviously not that market.

Somoza's Nicaragua was a principal country for LAAD's operations. In addition to interests in export-oriented cattle

---

* The profit rate, however, is not insignificant. In 1978, LAAD completed its sixth consecutive year of steadily increasing profits. Net earnings grew by 36 percent in 1978, to $511,000, representing a 13.2 percent on average outstanding common stock. LAAD even uses AID's low-interest loans to turn a nice profit: agribusiness affiliates that borrow from LAAD pay interest rates of up to nine percent.[48]

ranches, rice production, and American-style supermarkets, LAAD lent over $300,000, mostly from our AID tax money, to Industrias Amolonca. Industrias Amolonca was formed to use prime agricultural lands to produce black-eyed peas for stews and soups, and frozen, packaged vegetables such as okra for its major contractors, Safeway Stores and Southland (Seven-Eleven).[50]

portantly, the "Indian communities" are made up of economically and socially better-off mestizos.[52]

In order to determine AL-COSA's local impact, the Checchi investigation focused on the village of Patzicia. It found that the already better-off small farmers, mostly mestizos, who had some capital to begin with and who were "opportunistically entrepreneurial," had gotten the contracts.[53] Their increased in-

---

. . . agribusiness increasingly prefers to be the multinational marketer of crops supplied by smallholders under supervised credit schemes.

Amolonca employed a total of 26 people, 10 of whom were salaried managers and administrators. The capital invested per employee was a phenomenal $47,817 in a country where officially the rural unemployment rate ran between 20 and 32 percent and unofficially the rate was as high as 70 percent. Over three-quarters of the rural people earned less than $120 per year.[51]

LAAD's 1977 annual report boasts about ALCOSA: "a Guatemalan frozen food company" that supplies the U.S. supermarkets with okra, broccoli and cauliflower "grown by Indian communities." A late 1977 investigation by Checchi and Co., however, found that although ALCOSA might sound Guatemalan, it is an affiliate of the U.S. food multinational Hanover Brands. More im-

come has touched off a speculative land market in which the smallest landholders, mainly Indians, have lost their land and become seasonal laborers on farms growing cauliflower for AL-COSA. The net result, the evaluation concludes, is "an increase in economic inequality." The evaluation calls the harm caused to the poor Indian families by the dynamics of such an operation "ironic," since the ALCOSA field manager is considered "almost an Indianist."

In the eyes of AID, LAAD has proved to be a success—a success that should be copied in other parts of the world. In 1977, AID (as well as the World Bank) contracted with LAAD for advisory services for agribusiness projects in Afghanistan, the Philippines and the Sudan. In 1978, LAAD expanded its operations into the Caribbean and Chile with a fresh AID loan. One investment has already been made in a new affiliate of Hormel Meats in the Dominican Republic.[54]

AID connections with international agribusiness are not limited to LAAD. The chief administrator of AID also serves as head of the Overseas Private Investment Corporation (OPIC),† an insurance and lending agency that puts the U.S. government behind the foreign investments of such firms as Star Kist Foods in Ghana, Del Monte in Kenya (pineapples), and CPC International in Iran.[55] (For a more detailed discussion of OPIC see our response to Question 18 and the Primer.)

The World Bank and multinational corporations

One part of the World Bank, the International Finance Corporation (IFC),† was created to "act as a catalyst, to bring together private foreign and domestic capital and investment opportunities, and to facilitate investment with its own funds."[56] IFC provides loans for hotels and other profit-making ventures as well as for agribusiness. In some cases IFC takes an equity interest in such projects which it later sells to private interests.

An example of the kind of venture that IFC aids is Bud Senegal, started by the European affiliate of the Bud Antle Corporation—California's largest iceberg lettuce grower and now a subsidiary of Castle and Cooke (Dole)—as a joint venture with the Senegalese government.[57] Displacing a number of peasant farmers, the company established a large vegetable plantation near Senegal's capital city, Dakar. Chartered jets carry the produce grown under irrigation during the winter months to European tables. Three major IFC loans helped to start the venture. Other IFC loans have gone to food processors and export crop estates, primarily in Latin America and Africa.

In addition, the IDA, the soft-loan arm of the World Bank that is supposedly reserved for the "needy" governments, has apparently found some needy corporations. For example, a 1978 loan to rehabilitate commercial oil palm plantations in Zaire will, according to the Bank, "benefit three companies"—a subsidiary of the giant firm Unilever (known in the United States as Lever Bros.) and two Belgian firms.[58]

And benefit they will, in notable contrast to their Zairian employees. The plantation workers (3,500 jobs theoretically to be created by the project) will earn about $200 a year, or four dollars a week, low even for third world plantation work. The net annual income of the participating companies, however, is expected to be three million dollars at the time of the loan's maturity in 1987.[59]

In discussing its fears that the project's profitability might be reduced if unable to secure labor, the Bank's secret "gray cover" report on the project points out that better housing and social services for workers will be provided to "reduce the risk of labor shortage." Thus, while the World Bank talks publicly of its humanitarian motives, a reading of its private documents reveals that a better life for the poor is a goal only when it serves the economic interests of the real beneficiaries, in this case the multinational corporations.

Finally, the project completely overlooks the needs of Zaire's three to four million traditional small family farms. The rehabilitation of commercial oil palm plantations was selected because, the Bank says, it "offers the best prospects for future production increases at the least cost." Production maybe, development no.

Besides specifically assisting multinational giants with direct investments in third world agriculture, the Bank generally helps to promote the production of commodities in which multinational companies have trading monopolies: coffee, cocoa, rubber, oilseeds, tobacco and tea, to name a few. By promoting competition among the producing countries, the Bank helps to maintain a buyer's market for the trading companies.

We have responded to the question "do the aid agencies now focus on small farmers?" first by looking at how they define the small farmer. We found that their broad criteria most often include the middle strata or even the rural elite. Second, we discussed the actual village-level reality in countries in which these agencies operate. Where a few control most of the village's assets, as we detailed in the case of Bangladesh, the new technology or credit is most often captured by the rural elite— or at best the middle strata. Our conclusion is based on mounting evidence from people living and working at the village level in countries around the world.

Finally, the agencies' preoccupation with advertising their "small farmer" programs allows many to overlook the fact that both AID and the World Bank are directly and indirectly aiding giant agribusiness firms. For the hungry majority, the tragedy is not only in the diversion of food-producing resources but also in the direct threat posed to them by the power of the national elites, a power strengthened by their association with multinational corporations backed by U.S. tax dollars and the U.S. government.

8

QUESTION *Certainly there must be AID and World Bank projects that have helped farmers increase their productivity. Can't we say such projects help the poor and hungry?*

RESPONSE Official aid agencies assume that hunger can be alleviated by turning subsistence farmers into prosperous commercial growers. Their theory goes like this: peasant families in the third world produce only for their own consumption because they are bound by tradition and because their low productivity means they simply have nothing left over to sell. To break this pattern, peasants need the inputs necessary to improve their productivity and technical assistance to break out of traditional approaches. The result will be "marketable surplus"—something left over to sell—giving the family more cash income and allowing them to break out of poverty. At the same time, goes the theory, the society will benefit through the foreign exchange earned (if the products are exported) and/or by a greater supply of food for local urban residents.[1]

The real poor: the landless and nearlandless

This theory ignores several basic realities. First, it is simply not possible to become a commercial grower, even a nonprosperous one, without a minimum amount of land. It is precisely the poor majority who are deprived of this basic resource.

Sitting in Washington (or London or Bonn or Ottawa), aid policymakers apparently feel comfortable with the notion that most rural people in the third world are just small-scale versions of North American or Northern European yeoman farmers. Policymakers reason that what rural third world people need are packages of modern inputs (hybrid seeds, fertilizers, irrigation, extension services and market development) to increase their productivity. *But the real rural poor in most of the third world countries are not owner-cultivators.* Rather, they are tenant farmers, sharecroppers and day laborers—few with sufficient land and other productive resources to grow enough food even for themselves. They can survive only by selling their labor and that of their families. The number of these landless and nearlandless, as well as their percentage of the rural population, is increasing rapidly. In more and more countries they are the *majority*. A 1978 survey shows that in 20 Latin American and Asian countries, several of which are top recipients of U.S.-funded "development assistance," this group comprises 50 to 90 percent of the rural population.[2]

Whenever we have questioned AID and World Bank staff in Washington or in the field about what their programs will do for the landless, they seem at a loss. Sometimes they ramble on about job-creating welfare programs such as food-for-work that, at the very best, would imply perpetual funding to help a handful of the poor. (Refer to Question 14 for a discussion of the impact of food-for-work programs.) At other times, officials revive the arguments for "trickle-down," asserting that the millions of dollars for an irrigation dam or a farm-to-market road will generate more employment, a boon to the job-seeking landless.

No matter how much both small and large landowners increase their productivity, the landless will still go hungry. In Thanjavur, India, for example, new technologies have increased rice yields to three times the national average. But the underpaid landless day laborers who harvest the rice must survive by eating rats that thrive on the mountains of stored surplus rice.[3]

Productivity for whose gain?

The "new aid" supposedly takes into account the failures of the "green revolution."* The problem with the early green revolution strategies, it is acknowledged, is that the new input and technical assistance were inevitably cornered by the bigger landowners, thereby increasing the disparities between rich and poor —and leading to the ironic and tragic result of greater food production totals (per capita) and yet greater hunger.[4]

India and the Philippines, early targets of green revolution technology, are but examples. In both countries foodgrain productivity and production have increased dramatically. Yet, according to studies prepared for the World Bank, the per capita consumption of foodgrains in India in 1975-1977 had fallen below the level of 1970-1972 and even that of 1960-1962.[5] This decline occurred despite food production having outpaced population growth and despite steady increases in per capita income since at least 1960. In the Philippines, where rice production has almost doubled in the last decade, the population's average consumption of grain has sunk to the lowest in all Asia, with war-ravaged Cambodia the only exception.[6]

But, claim the aid agencies, we have learned: aid *now* targets the small farmers.

In raising questions about this "new aid," we noted in response to Question 7 that in the brutal

---

* For a full discussion of the impact of the "green revolution," please see *Food First: Beyond the Myth of Scarcity* (especially Part IV) by Frances Moore Lappé and Joseph Collins with Cary Fowler (Ballantine, revised 1979).

Table I.   Landlessness in the Latin American Region

Country	Landless as Percentage of Rural Labor Force	Landless & Nearland-less as a Percentage of Rural Labor Force
Argentina	24%	70%
Bolivia	38%	80-85%
Brazil	40%	59%
Colombia	20%	66%
Ecuador	28%	73%
Mexico	30%	50%
Peru	23%	60%
Costa Rica	35%	50%
El Salvador	38%	90%
Guatemala	29%	88%
Dominican Republic	35%	87%
Jamaica	24%	80%

—based on population figures (1975)

reality of an elite-dominated society, targeting the small farmer is often impossible, even when genuinely intended. In this response, we suggest that by stressing the needs of the "small farmer," aid agencies mislead people about who the *real* poor majority is in the third world, namely the landless and the nearlandless. A furthur point we wish to underline here is that a focus on small farmer productivity, even if it were successful with poor small farmers, is still a focus on productivity. Such a focus still raises crucial questions: Who benefits from this increased productivity? How will increased productivity help to alleviate hunger and poverty?

The hypotheses that we are testing as we study many different countries around the world are these: 1) helping small farmers increase their productivity is not synonymous with alleviating poverty and hunger; hunger and poverty can only be alleviated when a change in the structure of control over production includes all the disenfranchised—those with no or very little land, income and power; and 2) small farmers will be helped by increases in productivity to the degree that they effectively share in control over the acquisition of needed farm inputs and over the marketing of what they produce.

In other words, we are suggesting that increases in productivity will not *automatically* benefit either the small producers or the hungry, as official aid agencies seem to assume. Who gains hinges on the more fundamental question of control. To test our hypotheses, we at the Institute for Food and Development Policy are studying societies in which there have been increases in productivity by small farmers. We

Korea is cited as a prime example of the society-wide benefits resulting from a focus on increasing the productivity of the small farmer. Yet, under South Korea's repressive dictatorship, farmers are not allowed to organize cooperative marketing structures to serve their interests or even join together to petition the government for prices for their products that at least cover costs. Peasants find it hard to earn an adequate income and go deeply into debt even as their productivity has increased. [7] Increasingly mortgaged, the small farmer is vulnerable to foreclosure as a result of bad weather or other uncontrollable factors.

Taiwan. Massive fertilizer and pesticide use has dramatically increased productivity since the 1950s. But rural life is in decline.

. . . aid agencies mislead people about who the real poor majority is in the third world, namely the landless and the nearlandless.

are looking at a variety of countries such as South Korea, Taiwan, Venezuela, Cuba, the Philippines, Thailand and Malaysia.

While research to date does not allow comprehensive analysis of the benefits of increasing productivity to the small farmer in each of these societies, we are aware of certain trends that substantiate the hypotheses.

South Korea. Often South

One-fifth of all Taiwanese farm families have not been able to make enough to allow them to remain on the land. [8] Income of farm households is now 73 percent of nonfarm households. [9] Those remaining on the land must secure nonfarm income just to make ends meet, usually by sending daughters to work for low wages in foreign-owned electronics factories.

Philippines. The credit scheme Masagana 99, initially funded by AID, was launched in 1973. This government-sponsored credit program to increase the productivity of small farmers has further impoverished many of them. By 1977, the government announced that over 50,000 borrowers were being taken to court. Many were small farmers who had lost their crops due to natural calamities. Some were detained without trial and were forced to sell their farm animals or even their farms to repay the government loans. The primary beneficiaries of Masagana 99 have been the rural banks. Privately owned rural banks in the Philippines can borrow money from the Central Bank at one percent per annum and lend it to poor people at rates amounting to 100 percent per annum. The rural banking system nearly doubled its gross income in the first two years after the Masagana 99 project started.[10]

Another primary beneficiary of the Masagana 99 program is Planters Products, Inc., a company reportedly owned by cronies of President Marcos. Planters Products markets largely imported fertilizers, pesticides, herbicides and agricultural equipment. To participate in Masagana 99, farmers have had to use certified seeds. Certified seeds depend on massive use of the products sup-

Table II.   Landless and Nearlandless in Selected Asian Countries

Country	Landless as Percentage of Rural Labor Force	Landless & Nearlandless as a Percentage of Rural Labor Force
Bangladesh	28%	89%
India	32%	79%
Indonesia (Java only)	60%	89%
Malaysia	12%	51%
Pakistan	43%	88%
Philippines	55%	81%
Sri Lanka	54%	73%
Thailand	10%	50%

Source: Milton J. Esman and Associates, *Landlessness and Nearlandlessness in Developing Countries* (Ithaca, N.Y.: Rural Development Committee, Center for International Studies, Cornell University, 1973), pp. 182, 330. (Study contracted by AID, Office of Rural Development Project.) N.B. Most data were originally available in terms of household units; this study converted them to labor force units to provide greater comparability.

plied by Planters Products. The costs for these products have been greater than the benefits for many small farmers.[11]

Malaysia. In early 1980, authorities had to quell a farmers' riot in what is known as the "rice bowl of Malaysia," the state of Kedah. Some 10,000 farmers protested the low prices they have been getting for their rice and a subsidy program they say is benefitting the wealthier rice-millers.

The area has been the target of the Muda Agricultural Development Authority which has received at least $61.5 million from the World Bank. Covering 234,000 acres of irrigated land and including 70,000 families, the Muda irrigation scheme has been a "showpiece of economic development....(I)t aimed to serve national and local objectives by bringing the green revolution to Malaysia," according to the *Far Eastern Economic Review.*[12]

Measured in productivity increases, the Muda scheme is a grand success. This year the area is expected to produce a rice yield more than three times greater than before the project started. But gains from such increases by the 24 percent of the population who have to rent their land have been undercut by higher rents which have, in some cases, nearly tripled. And, even for the 34 percent who own their own land, rising costs of labor, tractor rentals and fuel mean that in real terms they are probably earning only about 75 to 80 percent of what they earned in 1975.

"The bulk of the economic surplus generated by the rice cultivation continues to flow out of the area," notes the *Review*. "Chinese millers and middlemen have little incentive to reinvest their profits in the area," and farmers' bank deposits are more likely to be invested in palm oil estates or urban property elsewhere, rather than in the development of Kedah.

What precipitated the 1980 riot was the government's decision to subsidize farmers with coupons instead of cash, as in previous years. The coupons were deposited by the government in government-run savings banks. In theory, the farmers would be able to get their money out in three months. In effect, according to the *Review,* the subsidy goes to the rice millers. Others gaining from the scheme are middlemen. Many farmers found they could not afford the cost and inconvenience of traveling all the way to a town and dealing with an unfamiliar institution—the bank—in order to cash the coupons. So, some farmers sold their coupons at a discount to middlemen.

Aid-financed small farmer credit schemes, even if not siphoned off by national and village elites, invariably take away what little power the small farm-

ers might have once had over their lives. Under the banner of "supervised credit," the farmer, frequently pressured or seduced to join the program, is obligated to use such-and-such inputs; credit is given in the form of fertilizers, seeds, pesticides, machinery, etc. Planting, spraying and harvesting practices are specified. The farmer does not have freedom to decide which inputs and practices are worth the cost or from whom to buy. Various extension and insurance programs are mandatory and the charges are deducted from the payment to him for the harvest. The sale of crops to the project authority (which may, in fact, be a multinational agribusiness corporation) or the government purchasing agency is usually mandatory. Failure to follow instructions or to fulfill the terms can be punished by taking the farmer's land.[13]

U.S. small farmers and increased productivity

We needn't go halfway around the world to consider the impact of a narrow productivity focus. Essentially, this has been the focus of U.S. agricultural programs since the mid-1940s. (Corn yields, for example, have tripled.) What has been the result of great boosts in productivity for small farmers? During this period of large productivity increases, half the farms in the United States—at the rate of 1,900 per week—have gone out of business and farm debt has ballooned to over

$135 billion.[14] Over the past 25 years, giant food corporations in the United States have increasingly relied on contracts with nominally independent farmers. Currently, roughly one-third of the American food supply is produced under corporate contract.[15] Many so-called family farmers are in reality closer to being hired hands in a corporate factory—only they go into debt to build and equip the "factory." The processor corporation has superior bargaining power. Many farmers producing under contract have achieved world-record levels of productivity and yet have little more than high costs and debts to show for it.

Just as in the third world, U.S. farmers have been (and are) at the mercy of the monopoly control of farming inputs as well as of banking, processing, and marketing.

To repeat, one hypothesis that we are testing is this: small farmers will gain from productivity advances to the degree that they can continue to organize to share control over the distribution of water and other farming inputs and over their marketplace return. In so many countries the opposite is occurring—most farmers have less and less control over the rewards of their production even though they might be producing more and more. Many governments deny them their civil rights to join together to improve their position.

There are some exceptions, however, that will be instructive to study in coming years. One of the newest exceptions is Nicaragua. Since the overthrow of the Somoza dictatorship, peasants are being allowed to organize. Peasant organizations will apparently help to decide how control over land and marketing will be reorganized.[16] Another country in which peasants may be gaining rather than losing control is Mozambique, which freed itself from Portuguese colonialism in 1975.[17] Farmland there is gradually being reorganized under the control of cooperative villages in which all who work have a say. An elected village-to-national decision-making structure is being established with the goal of directly involving peasants in policymaking for village development. It will be important to learn whether or not this emerging village-level democracy can be translated by the peasants into power at the national level to determine development priorities.

Similarly in China, since 1979, peasants' incomes have been increased by government policies to decrease the costs of farming inputs and to increase the prices paid to farmers for their commodities. Will this mean that Chinese peasants will move closer to the living standards of their urban counterparts?

Many important lessons concerning agricultural development for the benefit of rural people can be gained by studying both the successes and the setbacks in such societies.

9

If control over land and other resources is such an essential determinant of who benefits from their programs, are AID and the World Bank now promoting land reform and other means of redistributing control?

RESPONSE AID,† in a 1978 Agricultural Development Policy Paper and in a later Policy Determination, identified distribution of productive assets, especially land, as the major determinant of whether rural development benefits the poor or only an elite minority. "A highly skewed distribution of land...will adversely affect both improved equity and increased production, thereby rendering a broadly participatory agricultural production strategy virtually impossible to implement."[1]

What AID has officially ratified is what has been documented for years by development analysts —and, of course, well known by the rural poor themselves. What AID seems unable to do, however, is make its program priorities match its "policy determination." According to subsequent testimony by AID's Deputy Administrator, a mere six percent of the budget of Agriculture, Nutrition and Rural Development—in itself only a fraction of the agen-

cy's total budget—is devoted to "improved access and equitable distribution of assets, especially land, to the poor."[2]

This six percent contrasts with much higher allocations to programs that, according to the cited Policy Determination, will not benefit the poor majority: 26 percent to improve rural infrastructure; 28 percent to introduce new technology and to provide extension services to small farmers; 30 percent for marketing and storage, rural industries, and credits and inputs; and seven percent for agricultural production and planning analysis.[3]

Is it simply that the creeping bureaucracy of AID needs more time to catch up with policy determination? We think that there are good reasons to think not; the problem is more systemic.

Can't rock the boat

AID's Policy Determination says that it will consider supporting any *request* for assistance in land reform where there is a genu-

---

† See "A Primer: Some Essential Facts about the Aid Establishment" at the end of this book for an in-depth description.

ine commitment from the government. How many governments would issue such a request? Everything we know about land reforms that have worked teaches that there must be a fundamental shift in *power* in favor of the land recipients (whether individual or cooperative members) in order for them to benefit. Are current elites likely to ask the United States to assist in programs to challenge their power?

Official aid agencies at best might push for the parcelling of some land to some of the landless—if the large landowners are thought to stand in the way of modernization and are politically weak on a national level, or if there is sufficient "rural unrest" to threaten revolutionary change, or both. But it will only be accepted by local elites if the basic power status quo remains untouched. After such a top-down reform, leaving the national power structure intact—or even reinforcing it—and creating small individualized holdings with no unified power over inputs or marketing by the "beneficiaries," the poor might be slightly better off, or even *worse* off than before the reform.

Many peasant families in Venezuela found this to be the case after the land reform in the early 1960s. Peasants received parcels of land on the condition that they accept the government's credit for inputs and technical instructions, and that they sell their corn to a nearby processing company. Fifteen years after the land re-

form and after dramatic productivity increases, peasants who were the supposed beneficiaries of the reform told us that, based on their own investigations, their nutritional well-being was markedly *worse* than that of subsistence producers who had not received land from the government. And, the low government-set price they got for their products did not allow them to purchase an adequate diet or improve their communities.[4] Moreover, the reform "beneficiaries" discovered that the flour they had to buy from the company that bought their corn was much less nutritious than the handmilled cornmeal they had previously made themselves.

AID supports status quo reform

The type of reform that might be acceptable, indeed might be promoted, by an elite-controlled third world government is exemplified in Ecuador during the 1970s. M.R. Redclift, author of a book on peasant organization in Ecuador, studied the impact of AID-backed agrarian reform in that country from 1968 to 1975.[5]

During the 1960s, the Ecuadorian government began to identify land tenure patterns in the prime agricultural coastal region as a block to productivity. Owners of the large estates controlling a large part of the region were absent for much of the year, leaving their land in the hands of hired managers. The land was actually worked by tenants who lacked both the resources and the incen-

Tobacco harvest, Lilongwe Land Development Project, Malawi, funded by the International Development Association of the World Bank.

tive to improve productivity. Thus after 1970, the government began a reform program of distributing land titles to tenants. Some of these new owners were then able to form marketing cooperatives with the assistance of AID technicians.

The benefits of the reform were very unevenly distributed, according to Redclift. The government concentrated the bulk of credit for infrastructure and irrigation on a "select group of forty cooperatives." Concludes Redclift, "the main beneficiaries of AID's efforts were a highly select group of former tenants, whose possession of important natural resources proved attractive to the Ecuadorian State." The less fortunate former tenants "were forced to work for the others."

The reform also strengthened the power of the government. In the process of replacing the large estate owners with a handful of cooperatives, the government came to control the marketing and the processing of the crops produced.

Redclift also suggests that the reform did not challenge the structure of control over the land, except to get rid of some large estate owners who had shown little interest in agriculture anyway.

The cooperatives that emerged, Redclift notes, "were complementary to the large private estates producing sugar, bananas and coffee on the Coast. [They] represented no threat to the multinational companies like United Brands, which bought export crops from small producers at highly disadvantageous prices."

"in many countries, avoiding opposition from powerful and influential sections of the rural community is essential..."

Such an "agrarian reform," supported by agencies like AID or the World Bank, can have the effect of strengthening the position of an enclave of better-off producers, at the cost of forestalling possibilities for a more sweeping reform, motivated by an organized peasantry, and benefiting an entire rural population.

Land reform
à la the World Bank

The Bank's policy statements on land reform are strong. In a 1974 policy paper entitled "Land Reform," the Bank states that land distribution should play a role in determining loan recipients: "[the Bank] should give overt priority in lending to those countries and projects which meet land reform criteria...[the Bank] should not lend for projects if tenure arrangements are so bad that they frustrate the achievement of Bank objectives."[6] Such statements could easily mislead those who have not examined the flow of World Bank loans. Bank programs favor exactly the opposite kinds of countries—those such as Brazil, Indonesia and the Philippines where governments are brutally suppressing the efforts of rural people for land reform.

The Bank's 1975 Rural Development Policy Paper, however, clearly identifies the constraints within which it must live. In discussing how projects should deal with "the existing social system" it states that "in many countries, avoiding opposition from powerful and influential sections of the rural community is essential...."[7] We would suggest that it is for these reasons that Bank president Robert McNamara states that the Bank's agricultural program "will put primary emphasis *not* on the redistribution of income and wealth—as necessary as they [sic] might be in many of our member countries—but rather on increasing the productivity of the poor, thereby providing for a more equitable sharing of the benefits of growth."[8]

Promoting individual ownership as land reform

In its land reform policy paper under the heading "lending operations for land reform," the World Bank mentions only two projects: one in Tunisia which, in the Bank's words, "collapsed," and the other in Malawi, the Lilongwe development scheme. A central objective of the Lilongwe project has been the replacement of communal land tenure, common traditionally throughout much of Africa, with individual ownership.

Cheryl Payer, in her study "The World Bank and the Small Farmers," clarifies the danger to small farmers in such schemes billed for their benefit. The Lilongwe project is justified by the Bank as an answer to the need for a "more secure and lasting tenure system." Payer challenges this justification of individual land ownership. She points out that a number of observers have shown that

individuals have in fact sufficient security of tenure under traditional systems to improve the land and to plant cash and tree crops; and that the African system not only provides security to all members of the community but also has more flexibility in allowing adjustment of population to available land through migration, the fallow system, etc....registration of land to individual ownership *destroys* the security of traditional tenure forms....[9]

Thus African farmers have been generally "hostile to official attempts to change their tenure rights." In this case, specifically, Payer contends, there was no widespread demand for change on the part of the farmers. Payer quotes legal expert Rowton Simpson concerning the land registration law in Malawi: "There is no surer way of depriving a peasant of his land than to give him a title to it which is as freely negotiable as a bank note."[10]

The effect, if not the motive, of promoting individual ownership of the land is to lay the basis for a *market* in land. Payer believes that the development of a land market has been the motive.

Where land is bought and sold, two interrelated phenomena occur: control over the land is concentrated as those with more wealth are able to squeeze out the poorer farmers. Simultaneously, once land is bought and sold as an investment, there is pressure to reap the greatest possible profit from the investment. Thus, crops that bring the highest return in the international market are favored.

Payer quotes Montague Yudelman, later to become the World Bank director of agriculture and rural development, enthusiastically supporting change from communal to individual ownership in order to bring about "an effective land market." In 1964, examining Bank-supported tenure changes in the black reserves in Rhodesia, Yudelman noted that the result of such changes "would preclude emphasis on subsistence production and would ultimately lead to specialization of production and commercialization of agriculture." He also was aware that "the creation of a market for land will surely mean that there will be renter and rentier classes.[11]

Yudelman was not on the staff of the Bank at the time he praised this process. Undoubtedly, the Bank today would disassociate itself from such a summary of the impact of land registration. But the "land market" impact, so well described by Yudelman in 1964, is in practice what the Bank is fostering in virtually all of its rural schemes—the commercialization of agriculture, or in other words, the increased production and sale of crops with high value in international trade. But we have learned that the increasing commercialization of agriculture is a distinctly different goal from rural development. Productivity and the commercialization of high-value crops can expand while the welfare of rural people decline, as we explained in our response to Question 7.

Don't agencies such as the World Bank and AID have the sophisticated procedures and the professionalism to insure that money is not wasted? Aren't they more effective with money than small nongovernmental aid agencies?

RESPONSE This view of AID and the World Bank does not coincide with our findings. In our investigations in third world countries we repeatedly hear the Bank referred to as a "money pusher." Perhaps the World Bank's goal of stimulating exports from the industrial countries encourages big lending.* In addition, loan officers within the World Bank hold considerable power: they set target quotas for countries and judge subordinates on how well they find project outlets to fill those quotas. They often complain, we are told by Bank insiders, that there are not enough big projects.

Finding outlets for prodigious sums of foreign exchange isn't exactly conducive to Bank officers reflecting on the social consequences of projects they are planning. "Anyone who stops to raise such questions," we were told by one Bank consultant who has worked with almost every department of the Bank, "is considered an obstructionist—not a good team man."

Even some Bank employees have raised concerns about the Bank as a hasty spender. In late 1979, *Barron's* disclosed the findings of a draft report by the World Bank Group Staff Association. The report "denounces management for measuring effectiveness and productivity solely by the numbers of dollars loaned and projects processed and suggests that the Bank has become too 'output-oriented' at the expense of both the quality and the ultimate development impact of its work," reports *Barron's*.[1]

Similarly, AID's program in the African Sahel entails more dollars per capita than any other AID program in the world. One disillusioned AID officer said of the program: ". . . we have more money available than we are able to effectively use. . . No one has a chance to really stop and look at what is happening because of the constant pressure to get more

---

* See our response to Question 11.

funds on the bottom line for the next fiscal year."[2]

This "excess of funds syndrome," as many in the field speak of it, launches premature, large-scale projects when smaller-scale, slower-germinating projects would be at least less undesireable. This syndrome also lends itself to the perpetuation of extreme corruption in government. The *Wall Street Journal* reports that in Indonesia it is "authoritatively estimated" that 10 to 15 percent of the total outlay for Bank-financed projects (now running at over $500 million a year) is dissipated through "leakage."[3] Of the 15 World Bank Indonesian agricultural projects that have been operating for at least four years, the average cost overrun compared to appraisal forecasts is expected to be 76 percent.[4]

In Tanzania, a major part of a Bank-financed urban garden project was spent on a contractor for construction of storage facilities. A community worker who had worked closely with the project told us that the structure built with Bank support cost four times as much per square foot as a comparable one built by the participants themselves in a nearby similar project. (When we published the charge in 1979, the World Bank denied it, claiming the cost difference was minor.[5])

A House subcommittee investigating international financial institutions found that an urban development project funded by the Inter-American Development

Bank in Latin America included a community center and swimming pool-gymnasium "overdesigned for such purposes and...far more elaborate than might be found in affluent communities of developed countries."[6]

On a much larger scale, colleagues Betsy Hartmann and James Boyce report the Bank's willingness to throw in millions of dollars unnecessarily, even when the Bank knows that it will be pocketed by the wealthy and corrupt. In response to Question 7, we described an IDA-sponsored tubewell project in Bangladesh. There we stressed that on the local level the largest landowners gained from the aid-subsidized wells. The person who benefited the most by far from the project was not a landlord, however, but a businessman named Jahural Islam, reputed to be Bangladesh's richest citizen. (Mr. Islam prefers to reside in England.) It was his company that secured the contract to supply pumpsets for the tubewell project. Hartmann and Boyce report:

> In the process, the price tag on the pumpsets jumped to $12 million, although another company had reportedly offered to provide them at the World Bank's original cost estimate of $9 million. According to a report in the *Far Eastern Economic Review,* at this point the Dacca staff of the Bank urged that the project be postponed or canceled altogether, but they were over-

ruled in Washington. In the words of one official, Islam's extra $3 million was "easier than robbing a bank."[7]

As the largest single lender in most countries, the Bank can also undermine the efforts of smaller official and voluntary agencies that try to circumvent corrupt and exploitative structures by placing tight conditions on aid. No government will bother with such agencies when the Bank is ready to lend large sums without effective controls. In Bangladesh, we learned of one aid agency laboring for four years to design a $4.5 million funding to the Agricultural Research Institute and then, at the last minute, the World Bank came along and dumped in an additional $10 million to "beef up" the Institute.

The aid agency officers were horrified; they feared that this sort of sudden money would be bad for the Institute. Indeed, they argued, had more money been in order, they themselves would have arranged it. The Bank, we have often been told, tends to be a "reckless lender."

No accountability

A related and troubling issue is that of accountability. It would be naive to expect that such a powerful institution as the World Bank will or can effectively monitor itself. The Bank is in no sense a democratic or representative institution. It is accountable to no one but itself.

Bank documents are secret. The bank is virtually unstudied even by academics. No staff member will testify before any congressional or parliamentary hearings. Only recently has the Bank begun to go through the motions of evaluating the projects it funds. Of course, the evaluations are secret. Those who have seen some reports of the Bank's Operations Evaluations Department tell us that they were greatly "sanitized" when summarized for public release.

Evaluations are sometimes commissioned of outside consultants. But how independent can they be, given that their next contract might come from the Bank? We have learned of one such major evaluation which was critical. It was suppressed and the author ordered to "re-write." Public reports, we are told, must be upbeat in order to gain support in the congresses and parliaments of donor countries.

While in Bangladesh, informed foreign sources told us that a mission had recently flown in from Washington and pronounced the Rural Development I program (which we discussed in Question 7) a success "because it is based on sound principles" and declared that it should be expanded. Yet only the day before a Bangladesh government official had shown us an internal Bank memorandum indicting every aspect of the implementation of the project and concluding that the co-op system operates "excessively in favor of the more wealthy farmers."

Moreover, many local government negotiators of Bank loans often aspire to a position with the Bank in Washington, or at least a lucrative consultancy with the Bank. Are they about to question a Bank project?

Accountable to no one, the Bank is free to make whatever grandiose claims it wishes about the number of people who benefit from its projects. Mr. McNamara, for instance, would have us believe the Bank's agricultural and rural development program has "reached" 60 million people in the "poverty target group" by lending from 1975 to 1979. The Bank likes to count beneficiaries by counting the number of people living in the area where a Bank project is to take place. If two million people live in the area and half are said to be poor, then the Bank's public relations department simply assumes one million poor people will benefit.

Although the World Bank is blatantly unaccountable, this does not mean that responsibility cannot be assigned. The U.S. government has the greatest voting power—21.5 percent—of any member of the Bank.[8] U.S. taxpayers have directly contributed 28 percent of the funds to the International Development Association (IDA),† the "soft-loan" section of the Bank. Moreover, although the strictly commercial arm of the Bank does not get its capital from government subscriptions but from the public sale of bonds—many held by universities, pension funds and churches —the fact that governments back these bonds is an important factor in attracting private investors.

11

QUESTION

Even if most aid isn't going to agriculture and rural development or to the poor, doesn't it help to stimulate third world economies?

RESPONSE To understand how third world economies are affected by aid dollars, it must first be understood that a large part of the funds provided by AID† and all of the funds provided by the World Bank† are not contributions but *loans*, usually interest-bearing.

Even when a project designed almost entirely by an aid agency is a complete economic fiasco, the loans (often in no small measure spent on the handsomely paid consultants who dreamed up and directed the project) must be repaid—with interest. Similarly, an aid-financed project that merely enriches a relative handful of elite landowners and a multinational agribusiness company must be repaid by the national government and invariably a government that would not dare burden its well-off citizens with taxes.

Debt for development?

These "aid" loans, as well as those from private banks, contribute to what is becoming an almost unbearable debt burden for most underdeveloped countries. The third world debt burden has *quadrupled* in the last 10 years.[1] Debt-burdened countries are locked into an all-out emphasis on production for export in order to earn the foreign exchange needed to repay the debt.

Each year an ever-greater portion of aid coming into most countries must go to repay loans received in previous years—the classic "roll-over" treadmill. As early as 1973, over 40 percent of the official aid from all the industrial countries was consumed in repaying past "aid."[2] In 1977, Latin American countries paid more to the U.S. government than they received that year in new loans from both AID and the U.S. Treasury Department's Export-Import Bank.[3]† In 1978, more than 58 percent—$2.25 billion—of new borrowings from the World Bank (including its "soft loan" facility, IDA) went to cover the repayment and interest servicing of existing debt to the Bank.[4]

When debt payments by the underdeveloped countries to public and private lenders are combined, the total debt service burden of the non-oil-exporting

---

† See "A Primer: Some Essential Facts about the Aid Establishment" at the end of this book for an in-depth description.

third world countries just about equals the total flow of development assistance from all the industrial countries.[5] Debt service— estimated at $40 billion in 1979— is rising much faster than aid receipts (grants and new loans) and mounting faster than the ability to repay through increased exports. Over half of these payments go to private transnational banks such as Chase Manhattan and Bank of America.[6]

Many countries, such as Zaire, Peru, Bangladesh and Brazil, have surpassed what bankers consider a "tolerable" level in their debt-service ratio† (debt service/ export income). The private transnational banks, having clearly overlent to a number of such countries, now look to fresh aid agency loans to those governments as the only way to increase the cash flow sufficiently to get their money back. Again we must ask, *whom* are we aiding?

There is another consideration that led us to judge that our official foreign assistance is considerably less than a contribution. Many, if not most, aid projects require the local government to put up "counterpart funds"† amounting to 20 to 60 percent of the total cost of the project. Thus, a government's scarce financial resources—and considerable human ones, too—are tied up by "aid" projects.

An article in a World Bank periodical, intriguingly entitled "How Project Assistance Adds to Third World Woes," highlights this serious problem. The article notes that "Other, smaller projects, often entirely locally funded, will be deprived of funds or manpower resources to support the larger (internationally funded) projects."[7]

Aid to U.S. corporations

Loans and grants we know as "aid" are largely used to finance purchases of what the corporations in "donor" countries have to sell. Each year when the aid agencies go before Congress to sell their programs, their presentations begin with a spate of humanitarian concern. But the heart of their pitch is in trumpeting the value of foreign aid to U.S. corporations and the *American* economy. **About three out of every four dollars in the AID budget are used to purchase products and consultative services in the United States.**[8] (Many American universities fare particularly well through big-dollar AID contracts.) As for the World Bank and the regional development banks,† for every dollar the United States government pays in, about two are spent in the U.S. economy.[9]

During 1978, AID-financed purchases from over 3,500 U.S. corporations totaled more than $1 billion. The benefits, however, were captured by a handful of corporations. Almost half of the total, or $504 million, went to 22 megacorporations, including Cargill, Caterpillar and International Harvester.[10] Figures on World Bank disbursement for 1978 show that the Texas construction firm Brown and Root, Caterpillar, and Alcoa Conductor

are among the principal recipients of Bank contracts.[11]

Whether rural or urban, development is inevitably defined in terms of goods that cost large sums of money and must be imported. Like AID's infrastructural projects, Bank-financed projects are designed to be high-cost and make startlingly little use of local resources. Economist Judith Tendler, a long-time student of aid institutions whose 1979 study of aid-funded rural roads was cited previously, sheds light on a method in this seeming madness:

> The donor policy of financing foreign exchange costs of an infrastructure project made it desirable for project designers in both recipient and donor agencies *to maximize the import component*

of the project—either through the importation of equipment by a highway department or the contracting of international contractors from the industrialized countries, who normally use equipment-based construction methods...[12]

As a matter of historical record, one of the chief purposes of the capitalist industrial countries in founding the World Bank following World War II was to stimulate their export of capital goods. This primary purpose was stated in its charter. Current World Bank president Robert McNamara suggests that this purpose remains an impetus behind Bank activity today. "The developing countries offer export markets larger than those of Western Europe, Eastern Europe, the Soviet Union and China combined, and therefore they serve as locomotives or stimulants to our own sluggish economy."[13]

U.S.-based multinational corporations now export $22 worth of merchandise to third world countries for every dollar of bilateral aid to the third world. Third world countries have become significant markets for U.S. corporations, accounting for more than one-third of all U.S. merchandise exports by 1977.[14]

It comes as no surprise, therefore, that multinational corporations are in the forefront of lobbying efforts for aid programs.* One lobbyist for the giant FMC (Farm Machinery Corporation) told the *Baltimore Sun*, "We don't see foreign aid as a liberal issue, we see it as part of world trade and we are part of world trade. Clearly foreign aid is of interest to us."[15]

The question asks, "Doesn't aid stimulate their economies?" Our response is that while third world economies become burdened with ever heavier debts, the primary stimulation aid provides is to increase sales of a relative handful of corporations in the "donor" countries.

---

* For years big labor united with big business as the principal lobbyists for expanded aid budgets. In recent years, however, labor unions have begun to question whether many aid programs are not paying for the infrastructure for runaway plants; i.e., the trend by multinational corporations to move their factories out of the United States to low-wage labor sites in the third world.

12

Don't U.S. food aid programs channel American abundance to hungry people around the world?

RESPONSE Perhaps the most important fact to remember about the U.S. food aid program† is that the bulk of U.S. food aid is not given away. Over the years, about two-thirds of U.S. food aid has gone under Title I of Public Law 480 (P.L. 480).[1] Under the provisions of Title I, foreign governments take out long-term loans from the U.S. government to purchase surplus agricultural commodities. Thus, the bulk of what is called "food aid" is actually purchased by foreign governments *that then may do with it as they please.* Generally, the food is sold on the local market—meaning that those who can pay for it, get it. (The hungry, of course, cannot pay.)

Before we look at the impact of food aid, it is instructive to examine its purpose. The $30 billion worth of food shipped abroad as aid since 1950 is often presented as a clear expression of the generosity of the American people. Undoubtedly, the humanitarian intentions of ordinary Americans supporting food aid are genuine. But the actual motives behind the program are something else.

During different periods of time, the U.S. food aid program served many purposes for diverse interest groups, but at no time has its primary purpose been to feed the hungry. In fact, the humanitarian intent was not even written into the food aid law until 1966. From its very inception in 1954, the food aid program has been an extension of foreign policy, farm interests and corporate interests, which in most cases have been mutually supportive. Public records unequivocally show that U.S. policymakers have viewed the food aid program as a means to:

• rid U.S. markets of price-depressing domestic surpluses.

• open new markets for commercial sales of U.S. farm products and thereby offset trade deficits.

• provide support for U.S. military interventions in the third world.

• extend the reach of U.S. agribusiness corporations into food economies abroad.

• pressure foreign governments to accommodate U.S. economic and military interests.

The origins of food aid

The direct origins of Public Law 480 (P.L. 480, or simply

---

† See "A Primer: Some Essential Facts about the Aid Establishment" at the end of this book for an in-depth description.

food aid) go back to 1951. In that year, India made an emergency request to the United States for grain to stave off famine precipitated by monsoon failure. Since the end of World War II, India had embargoed exports of monazite sands, which contain thorium, a material necessary for the production of nuclear weapons. The U.S. government seized the threat of famine as an opportunity to have the embargo lifted. Congressman Charles J. Kersten (R-Wis.), put it bluntly, "In return for the wheat we are asked to give to India, the very least we should ask of India is that it permit the United States to buy some of these strategic materials. . . ."[2] The result was the India Emergency Food Act of 1951, the direct predecessor of Public Law 480.

Public Law 480 (later called "Food for Peace") passed in 1954 and addressed a crisis that was much closer to home than the Indian famine: the great American grain surplus. During the 1940s, U.S. grain production had grown by almost 50 percent while domestic consumption lagged well behind, increasing only about 30 percent. Higher crop yields, resulting from more fertilizers, pesticide and improved seed varieties, as well as from price supports which encouraged farmers to peak production, were creating enormous surpluses costing taxpayers $1 million per day just for storage.

The farm lobby did not want the surpluses put on the domestic market. If dumped on the world market, grain prices would drop by a dollar a bushel; the giant grain-trading corporations opposed such a disruption of their international commercial market. At its national convention in 1952, the American Farm Bureau, a group representing large and medium-sized farmers, proposed a solution. They suggested the creation of a secondary foreign market by allowing food-deficient countries to pay for American food imports in their own currencies instead of in dollars. Thus, while not interfering with the commercial dollar price demanded from higher-income countries, P.L. 480 permitted third world governments, which otherwise would not constitute a market at all, to buy surplus American food. In terms of exporting grain, P.L. 480 meant the United States could have its cake and eat it, too.

Food aid and local production

Even before we began our research on food aid, we had long been familiar with the claim that U.S. food aid shipments depress the incentive of foreign farmers to grow their own food. We were tempted to reject this conclusion simply because it sounded like an unfounded critique of welfare ("If you feed 'em, they won't want to work").

We did not understand an important distinction. Many critics were charging that if you give people food they will not *want* to grow food for themselves. The fact is that dumping large quantities of low-priced American grain in underdeveloped countries makes it economically *impossible* for the small domestic producers to compete. Unable to get a fair return for their grain, such producers are frequently forced to sell their land and become landless (and often jobless) laborers. A study in 1969 concluded that for every pound of P.L. 480 cereals imported, there was a net decline of almost one-half pound in Indian domestic production over the following two years, because of the reduced return to the farmer.[3]

South Korea has been the second largest recipient of U.S. food aid and has purchased more U.S. agricultural goods than any other underdeveloped country.[4] A basic purpose of the U.S. food aid, along with more than $13 billion in direct economic and military assistance to Seoul since the end of the Korean War, has been to

proached the costs of production.[5] Not surprisingly, Korea's rural population fell from one-half to slightly more than one-third of the total population between 1963 and 1976.[6] People lost their livelihoods and were forced to seek jobs in the cities. Pressure from the remaining farmers forced some increases in the government's mandatory rice purchase price in the 1970s, but prices still fall below production costs, according to the Korean Catholic Farmers Association.[7] (Farmers who have dared to circulate a petition asking the government to pay a fair price for their rice have been harassed, arrested and beaten, according to Association members we interviewed in 1979.)

Nonetheless, former U.S. Assistant Secretary of Agriculture Clayton Yeutter proclaimed,

---

. . . dumping American grain in underdeveloped countries makes it economically impossible for the small domestic producers to compete.

---

maintain a low-paid, "disciplined" labor force for use by export-oriented multinational corporations that dominate the South Korean economy.

The U.S. grain imported into South Korea has allowed the government to maintain a "cheap food" policy, undercutting many Korean farmers. Throughout the 1960s, prices that the government paid to rice producers barely ap-

"South Korea is the greatest success story worldwide of the Food for Peace Program (P.L. 480) in terms of contribution to the growth of that nation."[8]

Colombia provides another dramatic example of the effects of P.L. 480 shipments. Between 1955 and 1971, Colombia imported from the U.S. over one million tons of wheat that could have been produced more cheaply

Damota, Ethiopia, wheat harvest. The IDA has assisted with a project to provide fertilizers and improved seeds.

locally. The marketing agency of the Colombian government fixed the price of the imported grain so low that it undercut domestically-produced wheat. This dumping resulted in 50 percent lower prices to Colombian farmers. From 1955 (the first year of P.L. 480 shipments) to 1971, Colombia's wheat production dropped by 69 percent while its imports increased 800 percent. By 1971, imports accounted for 90 percent of domestic consumption.[9]

Moreover, two-thirds of the 407,550 acres that were pushed out of wheat production by subsidized wheat imports have not been replanted in other crops for local consumption. For example, the fertile Sabana de Bogotá Valley which once grew wheat is now used for cattle grazing—primarily for export.[10] Such feeding operations were abetted by P.L. 480 loans that went to subsidiaries of U.S. multinational corporations such as Ralston Purina, Quaker Oats, Pfizer, and Abbott Laboratories to build plants for processing feed and producing veterinary drugs. Large landowners now making greater profits on beef, flowers, and vegetables for export, expand their operations, evict their tenants and, in general, exclude more and more ordinary farmers from the land. Without land and without jobs, those needing food cannot buy the food aid. In this traditionally corn-eating country, the imported wheat goes to meet the "demand" of the "Americanized" minority who can afford processed, brand-name foods.

The impact of American food aid to Bolivia has been similar. [11] But an additional turn of the screw came in 1972, when the United States stopped accepting payments in local currency and started demanding dollars for food aid shipments, albeit on easy terms. Despite its rich agricultural potential and high rural unemployment, Bolivia had come to depend on United States imports, and local wheat production had stagnated. Millers had become primarily flour-importing companies because importing was more profitable than milling. Thus, even after local currency was no longer accepted to repay P.L. 480 shipments, Bolivia had to continue to import flour. The big difference, however, was that Bolivia was forced to use its scarce foreign exchange to purchase the flour in dollars, foreign exchange that might have gone to purchase what it could not easily produce itself, such as productive industrial goods.

Bolivia is an example of a country which has, as the U.S. Department of Agriculture would phrase it, "graduated" from P.L. 480 status to that of a regular commercial buyer. Such a graduation is not always by choice. To receive food aid, the recipient sometimes has to agree to purchase U.S. agricultural commodities on commercial terms in the future. Agreements for P.L. 480 food aid to the Dominican Republic, Egypt and South Korea have been tied to such commercial purchases.

Haiti is one of the countries from which we have received first-hand reports that food-for-work programs and other channels of food distribution act as a market disincentive for local production. In 1978, we received the following report from Haiti:

In theory, these foods are given as a supplement to the local diet and go directly to the poorest people. Thus, the food aid is not supposed to decrease the incentive for local production, since it bypasses the local marketing system. In reality, the P.L. 480 food is available in almost every market in Haiti and competes directly with locally-produced food. . . . I met one Haitian swine and chicken-feed processing owner. His source of grain for this operation for several years has been P.L. 480 food. He would not elaborate on his source of P.L. 480 food, but indicated that his purchase price has been decreasing each year and that last year he paid one dollar per 100-pound sack. [12]

Although the disincentive effect of food aid on local production continues to be debated, a 1975 U.S. government (General Accounting Office) research survey concluded, "Leading world authorities now indicate that such food assistance by the United States and other countries has hindered the developing countries in expanding their food production and thus has contributed to the critical world food situation."[13]

Market development: boon to corporations

In the first five years after it was passed, P.L. 480 succeeded in exporting over $5 billion worth of American grain, or 28 percent of all American agricultural exports. Even this was not enough, however, to unload U.S. grain surpluses. By 1959, the United States held its highest grain stocks in history. Merely responding to food aid requests was not enough. Policymakers decided to take an active role in creating markets. The goal spelled out in the preamble to P.L. 480 included these words: "...to develop and expand export markets for United States agricultural commodities." The goal was clear; the question was how to achieve it.

Part of the answer, policymakers thought, was "development assistance." Assistant Secretary of State W.L. Clayton testified that World Bank financing for capital goods from the industrial countries "would certainly be...very good ...for U.S. agricultural exports, because as you help develop them (underdeveloped countries) industrially, you will shift their economy to an industrial economy, so that I think in the end you would create more markets for your agricultural products."[14] Added to this, P.L. 480, by allowing countries to import food *without* using dollars, until 1972, made it more likely that poor governments would have dollars available to import U.S.-manufactured capital goods for light industrialization.

The other part of the answer was direct support to U.S. corporations. Between 1959 and 1971, P.L. 480 provisions allowed up to 25 percent of the local currency generated by sales of U.S. food aid to be lent at low interest rates to U.S. corporations in order to finance their entry into a foreign country. Eldridge Haynes, Chairman of Business International, the service organization for multinational corporations, told the House Committee on Agriculture of the need to expand the U.S. food processing industry into the underdeveloped world in order to create a commercial demand for American agricultural exports.

"We are not exporting bread," he testified. "We are exporting wheat. Somebody has to turn it into bread. If they do not, if there are not facilities to make bread, it will not be consumed."[15] Haynes said the same is true of American tobacco and cotton. He suggested, therefore, that U.S. companies get "Cooley loans" to invest in plants for making cloth, cigarettes, and other products from agricultural commodities. These so-called "Cooley loans" were named after the House Committee on Agriculture chairman, Rep. Cooley (D-North Carolina). During the 12-year period from 1959 to 1971, P.L. 480 directly subsidized 240 private American and foreign businesses overseas through the Cooley loan program. The U.S.

government loaned $419 million worth of local currencies collected by U.S. embassies in repayment of previous food aid shipments, making it possible for companies in 31 countries to start or expand abroad with little or no capital outlay.[16] In India alone, Cooley loans have gone to Wyeth Labs, Union Carbide, Otis Elevator, Sylvania, Rockwell International, Goodyear, CPC International, Sunshine Farms, First National City Bank, the Bank of America, and American Express, among others.

In 1972, when P.L. 480 repayment arrangements were changed from local currency sales to dollar sales, Cooley loans were changed into Private Trade Entity loan form. Under this loan program, the U.S. government now grants credits to American companies overseas to buy agricultural commodities in the United States. The overseas subsidiaries then use the proceeds from local resale of the products for their own financing.[17]

Building a feedgrain market: the case of Cargill, Inc.

In 1968, Cargill, Inc.—the multibillion dollar grain con-

AID advisor and South Korean executive in front of bags of flour purchased with Cooley loans.

glomerate—decided to build a complete poultry operation in South Korea, breeding chicks, producing chicken feed, and retailing chicken. The U.S. government—i.e., the American taxpayers—provided 95 percent of the financing for what looked like a very profitable operation. Almost $500,000 came as a Cooley loan. An additional $1.9 million loan from the U.S. government came to Cargill under the Private Trade Entity provision of P.L. 480.

This huge government subsidy, however, was not enough for Cargill to succeed. By 1972, the Cargill operation was in trouble. Cargill had used all possible P.L. 480 credits for importing grain. Cargill approached its friends in the U.S. government to persuade South Korea to relax domestic price controls and import restrictions that interfered with its feed-grain import operations. The State Department instructed the embassy in South Korea to see that the "poultry and livestock industries" received special consideration from the government. Finally, when all else failed, Cargill sought and received a deferment of payment on its two P.L. 480 loans from the U.S. government.[18]

P.L. 480 credits also enabled Ralston Purina and the Peavey Corporation to establish poultry operations in South Korea. The net effect has been to make South Korea heavily dependent on imported feed. Whereas South Korea had previously imported no feed grain, it imported about one million tons from the United States by 1974.[19] Furthermore, by 1974, when South Korea had become dependent on American feed-grain imports, the United States raised the price to three and one-half times its original (1970) price.

Building a wheat market

P.L. 480 has also succeeded in creating markets for wheat among the world's original rice lovers. P.L. 480 "was the best thing that ever happened to the wheat industry," observed one market development specialist, pointing to the tremendous increase in wheat consumption in such countries as Japan, Taiwan and South Korea. Wheat aid credits to the Chiang Kaishek government in Taiwan allowed it to export the people's staple, rice, while it exhorted the population to embrace the new diet by such slogans as "eating wheat is patriotic."[20] South Korea now has 7,000 bakeries, and Koreans eat Italian-style noodles made from wheat flour.[21] "We taught people to eat wheat who did not eat it before," bragged an official from the U.S. Department of Agriculture.[22]

P.L. 480 has perhaps proved that people like what they eat, rather than eat what they like. At any rate, American corporations have taught people to eat what they, the corporations, have to sell. This achievement was lauded in 1974, before the Senate Foreign Relations Committee, in testimony by former Secretary of Agriculture Orville Freeman

Wheat field spraying in India; wheat harvesting in Pakistan.

(now president of Business International—the same organization whose chairman, 17 years earlier, had urged the use of P.L. 480 to create markets for American agricultural exports). Freeman noted, "In the last seven years, our agricultural exports to Taiwan have climbed by 531 percent and those to [South] Korea by 643 percent because we created a market." P.L. 480 "makes very good sense," he added.

But it does not make such good sense for South Korea. The country as a whole has become heavily dependent on the highly volatile international market for grain—dominated by only five multinational corporations. Nor should Americans forget the political repercussions in our own country of collaborating with such corrupt regimes; e.g., the attempts by Korean grain merchant Tongsun Park to bribe members of the United States Congress to support even more food to the Korean dictatorship.[23] Tongsun Park maneuvered his way into a key middleman position, receiving substantial commissions for arranging sales between U.S. rice exporters (Connel Rice and Sugar, and Rice Growers Association of California) and the Korean government. He then used this fortune to buy influence in Washington and in various state governments. He bribed Rep. Otto Passman (D-Louisiana), a member of a House appropriations subcommittee which oversees the U.S. aid program. He also gave sub-stantial cash gifts to the governor of rice-producing Louisiana, Edwin Edwards. Due to his dealings with Tongsun Park, California Congressman Richard Hanna was convicted of defrauding the United States.

In spite of the Koreagate scandal, South Korea has continued to receive substantial quantities of P.L. 480 commodities under Title I: $59.5 million in 1978, and $40 million in 1979; $40 million has been proposed for 1980.[24]

Food as a weapon

While commercial forces worked from one end, broader political and military considerations influenced the P.L. 480 program from the other end. Thus, while our food aid has been distributed to 130 countries over the course of its history, at any particular period a few strategic countries have been the dominant recipients. Of these select few, U.S. military allies have been most favored: Israel and Turkey during the 1950s; South Korea, Taiwan and Pakistan throughout; and South Vietnam and Cambodia during the period of U.S. military intervention in Indochina.[25] By 1973, almost half of all U.S. food aid was going to South Vietnam and Cambodia. Between 1968 and 1973, South Vietnam alone received 20 times more food aid than was received during the same period by the five African countries most seriously affected by the Sahelian drought.

In 1980, U.S. food aid remains highly concentrated.

QUESTION 13

Hasn't U.S. food aid been reformed so that food for the hungry is now the top priority?

RESPONSE The first food aid† reform effort began in 1974. With many congresspersons outraged that almost half of all food aid credits were going to military allies in Indochina, Congress approved an amendment requiring that 70 percent of all food aid go to countries hit hardest by food and oil price increases. To remain within the letter of the law and still provide the same level of support for Vietnam and Cambodia, the administration simply raised the amount of food aid by $600 million.

In late 1975, Congress passed a new foreign aid assistance bill. Added to the new food aid bill were two amendments, both supported by many citizens who would like to see America's food bounty help the hungry abroad. The first amendment decreed that 75 percent of P.L. 480 loans must go to countries where the annual per capita gross national product (GNP) is $300 or less (the 1980 limit was $625). The second states that food aid cannot be given to any government that "consistently violates recognized human rights" of its citizens.

In 1977, Title III, "Food for Development," was added to the food aid law. Under this provision, the United States forgives repayment of food aid loans if the recipient government uses the proceeds from its sale of the food to undertake development programs in agriculture, nutrition, health services and population planning.

Let's examine carefully the new faces of food aid.

At least two false assumptions appear to be at work behind this amendment. First, the assumption that per capita GNP figures tell us anything about hunger is false. The annual per capita GNP of Brazil is $1,140, yet the majority of its 110 million people are undernourished. By contrast, the per capita GNP of China is $380, yet very few in China go without at least the minimum they need. Cuba has about the same per capita GNP as Brazil but since 1973, Cuban nutrition problems result more from overeating and bad dietary habits than from starvation. South Africa has a per capita GNP of $1,270, yet for the majority of the black population the figure is $360; many of them are hungry.

The second false assumption is

---

† See "A Primer: Some Essential Facts about the Aid Establishment" at the end of this book for an in-depth description.

Banana harvest along the Richamba-Guayaquil highway, Ecuador, which was built and funded by the IDA.

that the GNP criterion can help us judge which government would use food aid to help the hungry. Bangladesh has an annual per capita GNP of $110 while Haiti's GNP is about $200; yet we have learned that food aid in these two countries is more likely to hurt than to help the hungry.

The second 1975 amendment to P.L. 480, stating that food aid cannot be given to any government that "violates recognized human rights," contains a gaping loophole: a government widely known to be violating human rights can still receive food aid by simply agreeing to sign a special clause stating that the food aid will directly (or indirectly through the sale of food) help the needy. In late 1977, for instance, the Carter administration determined that Bangladesh was indeed a human rights violator. Did this mean a cutoff of food aid? Not at all. After months of administrative wrestling with the amendment and intense lobbying by the Bangladesh government, a deal was arranged. Bangladesh officials simply signed the special clause promising that they would use the food aid to help the hungry. They then received $56 million in food aid.[1]

The "helping the hungry" loophole has been similarly invoked for other governments which the State Department has classified as violators of human rights—including the dictator-ships in South Korea and Indonesia.[2] Moreover, Title II food aid—that which is channeled through voluntary agencies—is exempted from the human rights review amendment on the demonstrable specious grounds that Title II by definition helps the poor.[3]

By 1979, Title III agreements were worked out with Bangladesh, Bolivia, Egypt, Haiti,* and Honduras. But why would development programs financed under the new Title III provision be any more beneficial for the hungry majority than already functioning AID development programs whose negative consequences we have described previously? We have no reason to believe that they would be.

A high-level task force on food aid, mandated by the foreign aid legislation in 1977, completed its report for the Secretary of Agriculture in 1978. The report lauds the "maximum flexibility" offered by the food aid program in serving U.S. objectives. "Some programs are motivated in large part by our desire to further what are very clearly foreign policy interests," the report states. Eight countries are cited as examples—four of them in the Middle East. South Korea is also included as one of the eight; there, according to the task force, the large volume of food aid amounted to "a quid pro quo for that country limiting its textile exports to the United States."[4]

---

* At this writing Haiti has now refused to accept Title III because of the condition that it would have to make public its accounts.

To answer for yourself this question about whether food aid has been reformed, turn back to Chart IV listing the 10 countries that receive over half of all U.S. food aid. Are the majority of these countries among the world's poorest? No. Are the majority of the countries among those whose governments *you* would trust to get food aid to the hungry? Probably not.

QUESTION **14** *What happens when food aid goes to a country where the majority of the people are hungry?*

RESPONSE Bangladesh is the fourth largest recipient of U.S. food aid.† Most people think that food aid to a country with so many hungry people surely must be helping the country.

Today, one-third of Bangladesh's sizable food aid comes from the United States. Since 1974, about 90 percent of U.S. food aid to Bangladesh has been under Titles I and III of P.L. 480, which provides dollar credits to buy the U.S.-produced food. The government of Bangladesh, therefore, has virtually total control over what it does with the food. Like most purchasers of Title I food aid, the Bangladesh government sells most of it through a ration system that allows cardholders to buy a portion of their food at a substantial subsidy. The government then uses the proceeds from these sales for general budgetary support.[1]

Our colleagues Betsy Hartmann and James Boyce found that most of this food goes to those who could afford the regular market price—members of the urban middle class.* Conservative World Bank figures confirm their observations: 27 percent of the food aid goes to police, military and civil services and to employees of large enterprises; 30 percent goes to predominantly middle class cardholders in six major cities; and nine percent goes to supply mills for grinding flour for urban bakeries.[2] The few ration cards held by the marginally employed living in Dacca's slums were revoked in 1975 by the government.[3]

While 85 to 90 percent of the people of Bangladesh live in rural areas and many are undernourished, a mere one-third of the rationed food grains are allotted to rural families. In theory, rural ration cards allow for the purchase of half the amount of subsidized food allotted to an urban cardholder. In practice, rural cardholders can buy even less—in part because fulfillment of their allotment depends on the food left over after the urban allotments. Moreover, rural ration dealers sell much of the food they receive on the black market and pocket the cash; a dealership is a coveted political favor.[4]

---

† See "A Primer: Some Essential Facts about the Aid Establishment" at the end of this book for an in-depth description.

* For an in-depth report, see their book *Needless Hunger: Voices from a Bangladesh Village,* available from the Institute and described on the last pages of this book.

AID economist Joseph Stepaneck estimates that in practice "approximately 80 percent of the rationed-supplied food serves those with cash in towns and cities."[5] The government's concentration of food aid on the urban middle class is deliberate. The ration system is designed, in the words of a 1976 U.S. Embassy cable, "...to keep potentially active Dacca dwellers supplied with low-priced food grains."[6] "Active, " of course, is a euphemism for politically active.

embassy in Dacca acknowledged in a 1976 cable to Washington that "...the incentive for Bangladesh government leaders to devote attention, resouces and talent to the problem of increasing domestic food-grain production is reduced by the security provided by U.S. and other donors' food assistance."[9] This reduced incentive is welcomed by the Bangladeshi government. It is widely understood that to increase food production as well as to ensure access to the food pro-

---

"approximately 80 percent of the rationed-supplied food serves those with cash in towns and cities."

Food aid fails to feed Bangladesh's hungry; it also helps perpetuate hunger. Earlier we pointed out that the Bangladesh government has neglected agriculture, increasing the budget allotted to agricultural development by only five percent in real dollars between 1972 and 1977.[7] Food aid, many observers agree, is fundamental to that neglect. In the words of a Swedish International Development Agency (SIDA) evaluation of rural and agricultural policies of the Bangladesh government, "Food aid has, in short, enabled the government to continue with its policy of neglect of agriculture (and of land reform), a policy which has forced the government to rely more and more heavily upon imported food...."[8] Even the U.S.

duced would require a thorough restructuring of control over productive resources. That this is the last thing the military dictatorship wants is fully demonstrated by the brutal police and army repression it employs to crush popular movements by and for the poor majority.

Finally, the case of Bangladesh illustrates that those who believe that "humanitarian" stipulations on food aid legislation will ensure that food gets to hungry people overlook one central fact: food aid helps to finance a narrowly based, unpopular and, therefore, militarized government. Revenues from the sale of food aid through the Bangladesh ration system provide roughly one-fifth of the country's operating budget.[10] Of this operating

Commercial harvesting of radish crop for export in Kalihati, Bangladesh.

budget, 27 percent goes for "defense, justice, and peace."[11] The operation of jails falls under that budget heading. Amnesty International estimates there are 10,000 to 15,000 political prisoners held under "inhuman conditions."[12] Some of the food aid revenue which flows into government coffers undoubtedly goes to the 12,500-man militarized police Special Task Force trained for "special drives and mopping-up operations" against civilian dissenters.[13]

The Bangladesh government recognizes how much its own survival depends on food aid and wants the aid to continue. "Today it would be a budgetary disaster for the Bangladesh government if domestic production increased so much that the foreign donors refused to supply food aid," notes the SIDA evaluation cited above.[14] Thus government officials underrepresent actual harvests in order to strengthen their case for food aid. According to some estimates,[15] grain harvests are, in fact, adequate to feed the entire population. (This does not take into account the considerable non-grain production and the barely tapped rich agricultural potential.*)

---

* Bangladesh is becoming a "truck garden for the Middle East," air-freighting, in 1978, over 300 tons of fresh vegetables and fruits. In 1979, approximately $20 million worth of fresh fish was flown from Bangladesh to London—the profits in Bangladesh going to a few well-off merchants and not to the poor fishing people.[16]

QUESTION 15

What about food-for-work projects? Don't they also contribute to building roads and irrigation works that help the country achieve food self-reliance?

RESPONSE Most people in aid "donor" countries are conditioned to believe that what causes hunger in the third world is the lack of modern technology and the inefficient use of available resources. It is thought that what is missing are the roads, marketplaces, irrigation, storage facilities and other economic infrastructure which make commercial development possible, and the technologies which make agriculture more productive.

If one's focus is on the inadequacy of such things, then food-for-work projects seem like a perfect solution to hunger. The intent of such projects is to use food aid to pay jobless people to build infrastructure. It is thought that the individual workers benefit through the food payment while the society as a whole gains through the improved roads, water systems or buildings for agricultural research.

But does "society as a whole" ever gain in countries where wealth and power are tightly held? We think not. We have found that food-for-work projects, at their best, provide substantial and enduring advantage to those at the top with no long-term benefit to those at the bottom.

An AID-sponsored study makes the following observation about rural works projects that invariably use food-for-work aid: "Such projects (e.g., the building of a farm-to-market road) provide income to rural workers for a specified period, but do nothing generally to change the fundamental economic conditions that produced unemployment in the first place. At the same time, such projects tend to provide long-term benefits to landlords who, in this example, use the road to gain access to local markets."[1] Yet AID continues to promote food-for-work projects.

In Bangladesh, much of the 10 percent of U.S. food aid given under Title II of P.L. 480 is earmarked for food-for-work projects. Reports from a development worker in Bangladesh reveal that such projects are actively promoted by the rural elites. The Union Councils, the lowest administrative elected body (corresponding to several villages designated as one unit), are controlled by the large landowners of the area. Those who sit atop this

Rice harvest, Central Luzon, the Philippines.

local political, social and economic hierarchy design and submit project plans to the governments's Office of Rural Development. Our local informant explained why: "Not only do they [large landowners] get the benefit of improving their land and their friends', but also there's tremendous scope for using the power of patronage that it gives them. And also there's the possibility of diverting some of the resources without doing any work at all, which happens to a large extent."[2]

Unfortunately, the use of U.S. food aid to enhance the power of both an urban and rural elite is

dent, etc. Besides owning vast tracts of land, "the family" speculates in coffee and controls all the illegal tree-cutting in the area. When CARE entered the village with a food-for-work soil conservation project (using U.S. food aid), it came as no surprise that "the family"was the local administrator of the project and chose who would work on the project. "The family," through the auspices of the community council president, is also responsible for seeing to the actual food distribution.

. . .food-for-work projects, at their best, provide substantial and enduring advantage to those at the top . . . .

not unique to Bangladesh. Over the past several years, we have received numerous reports and letters from around the world questioning whether or not food aid really benefits the hungry. In 1978, for instance, we received several communications from American missionaries in rural Haiti. Independent of one another, they decried food-for-work programs using P.L. 480 Title II aid. One wrote:

In the village where we are living, for example, one family controls all the community and government offices including judge, mayor, community council presi-

To the CARE people this project is a good grass roots effort, but in reality it is not helping those peasants in the area who really need it. CARE, for example, believes that the workers are mostly landless peasants. We have surveyed nearly all of the workers on the project and have yet to find any landless peasants. The workers must work three days a week on the project, one day on the road for the community council and one day in the garden of one of the community leaders (i.e., "the family"). Thus the projects take the farmers away from their own plots for five days of the week.

Seasonal food-for-work projects are obviously no long-term solution to the unemployment that lies at the root of hunger. Moreover, in the opinion of some observers with whom we have spoken, the main function of such projects is to take the edge off a potentially explosive rural situation by providing a few jobs during the slack agricultural season.

A recent study by the United Nations stressed that food-for-work programs "...lend themselves to misappropriation of grain, misuse of funds, false reporting of works, creation of a new class of profiteers, poor quality construction, etc."[3]

Food-for-work projects now in vogue with many aid agencies are no exception to the lesson that we have had to keep learning and relearning: no outside donor's remedy inserted into an economic and political structure in which a few are in control can genuinely benefit those at the bottom. Food-for-work, like food aid and official "development assistance," actually strengthens the structures that generate hunger.

16

QUESTION

What about emergencies? Aren't there times of crisis—a flood, a crop failure, or war—when food aid is essential to prevent massive starvation?

RESPONSE Food aid is useful and can alleviate suffering only when it is in response to a short-term emergency, such as a severe drought or a flood that actually destroys food supplies, or to assist refugees.

We have come to think of the above statement as a working hypothesis, given the mounting evidence of the negative impact of food aid around the world. Rather than assuming that food aid *must* be helpful, we now think that the opposite assumption is more appropriate. Only by assuming that food aid will become part of the problem is a food aid program in response to a genuine emergency likely to be carried out with a great deal of care and knowledge of the local situation. In such an emergency, food aid should be given only after all means of garnering food within the afflicted country have been pursued, including rationing and measures to prevent hoarding. A more appropriate form of "food aid" in many instances would be the donation of transportation to help a local government move the necessary food from one agricultural area within the country to the emergency site.

It must be remembered that even in disaster-stricken countries there is seldom an absolute shortage of minimum supplies.

We have learned that even, or especially, in times of emergency, food aid can enhance the security of the rich and powerful to the detriment of the poor majority.

Ethiopia. During the final two years (1973-1975) of the U.S.-supported Haile Selassie regime, some 100,000 Ethiopians died of starvation due to drought. At least half the amount of grain needed to keep those people alive was held in commercial storage facilities within the country.[1] In addition, Emperor Selassie's National Grain Corporation itself held in storage 17,000 tons of Australian wheat which it refused to distribute. While commercial interests thrived by selling hundreds of tons of Ethiopian grain, beans and even milk to Western Europe and Saudi Arabia, the Ethiopian government received 150,000 tons of free food from aid donors. Government officials at all levels withheld stored food from the market, awaiting higher prices even as "...peasants could be seen starving within a few kilometers of grain storage.'' At one point, the Ethiopian officials offered to sell 4,000 tons of stored grain to the United States with the idea that the United States could then donate it back for relief inside the country.[2]

Upper Volta. Reports from local observers reveal at least 76 percent of the relief aid during the 1976 drought and subsequent political ''unrest'' was distributed to the better-off dwellers in the capital city and the largest provincial towns, leaving very little for the hard-hit rural areas.[3] At the same time, moneylenders-cum-merchants exported the grain they collected from debt-shackled peasants to the Ivory Coast.

In some incidences, extreme official corruption and callous disregard for life in countries receiving U.S. food aid have been cited by the U.S. government as reasons to stop food aid programs.

Ghana. In 1977, the U.S. government suspended the Title II emergency food distribution program, which was intended to provide relief for drought victims in Ghana's Upper and Northern Regions. According to the U.S. AID examination report of the program, ''Large quantities of food provided under the emergency program did not reach the high-priority recipients because of unexplained losses in transit, diversion, and issue to other than the most needy population.''[4] In four of the districts of Ghana's Northern Region, the report explains that ''. . .40 percent, 49 percent, 14 percent, and 25 percent respectively of the U.S.-provided grain was distributed to Government of Ghana employees.''

Food aid disaster

In visiting Guatemala, in 1977, we learned that even in times of natural disasters, food aid can undermine the livelihood of poor local farmers.

The terrible 1976 earthquake hit many small Guatemalan farmers who, prior to the earthquake, had exceptionally large harvests. Following the earthquake, they needed cash to help rebuild their homes and farms. To get that cash, these farmers needed to sell part of their stored corn and other grain.

Immediately following the earthquake, however, food aid from the United States almost quadrupled. CARE and Catholic Relief Services (CRS) handled most of the distribution. This increased availability of free food from the United States was one factor which helped to lower the prices for locally-grown grain, just when farmers most needed cash for their grain.[5] As a result, food aid *stood in the way* of reconstruction.

Even when the Guatemalan government finally asked voluntary agencies to stop bringing grain into the country, the food aid kept coming. CARE and CRS simply switched to grains preblended with other foods such as dry milk, since the ban specified ''grain.'' One year after the earthquake, U.S. food aid was still 69 percent above pre-earthquake levels.

Sorghum crop, Koro, Upper Volta. The IDA has financed programs to "improve agricultural techniques."

Ironically, two other voluntary organizations attempted to counter the ill effects of the indiscriminate distribution of free food. Oxfam gave a special loan to a cooperative in the stricken Chimaltenango area that had been organized earlier with the help of World Neighbors. The loan was used to buy crops from the farmers at a price above the depressed level and to establish a grain bank to help stabilize sinking grain prices. The scheme helped the farmers in the area get the cash they needed to rebuild their lives.

William Rudell and Roland Bunch, who have long experience with rural cooperatives in Guatemala and who were on the scene at the time, told us that even where there was a need for food during the first days following the earthquake, the food could have been bought from areas in Guatemala that were not affected by the earthquake. Such purchases would have been a boost to farmers in those villages. Moreover, supplies from within the country could have been *curtailed* more easily once farmers in the recipient villages had dug out their stored harvests. Bunch commented, "If the Guatemalans were sending wheat into the United States this year as their own version of a P.L. 480 donation and giving it out to American consumers, American farmers would be screaming bloody murder about it."[5]

Interestingly, it was the local people who most counseled against the distribution of free food and free materials. Instead, they advised the outside agencies to provide building materials and to sell them at subsidized prices. Oxfam, World Neighbors and U.S. AID did just that—with notably positive results.

Where disasters destroy rather than bury food supplies, all the lessons inherent in the Guatemalan food aid disaster might not apply. Yet, even in genuine short-term emergencies, relief food should be purchased, as much as possible, from local and national producers whose families' livelihood depends on selling their grain.

In addition, we must note the insensitivity of CARE and CRS to the harmful effects of the U.S. food aid programs they were administering not only on prices, but also on the basic ability of local communities to cope with disaster using their own resources, knowledge and leadership. Because so many people had to stand in line waiting for free U.S. food, it was hard for local farmers to find the labor to harvest their wheat. Bunch noted how the continuation of food aid handouts undermined the genuine leadership in the community: "Largely because of the giveaways, the villagers began to turn more to leaders who could produce free things, whether they were honest or dishonest, rather than turn to the leaders they'd been putting their trust in for years...Groups that had worked together previously became enemies over the question of the selection of recipients for free food."[7]

17

Are you proposing that chronic food aid be terminated?

RESPONSE Yes. In evaluating our response, please keep in mind these facts.

• U.S. food aid is not focused on those countries where there is the greatest hunger and the least local productive potential. It is focused on countries like Bangladesh, South Korea, Indonesia and Pakistan, because the U.S. government perceives the governments of those countries as allies to U.S. corporate and Cold War interests.

• Most U.S. food aid is *bought* by the recipient governments which then sell the food to their own people. Funds raised through the sale of food aid serve as general budgetary support, including maintenance of the police, military and bureaucracy necessary for unpopular regimes to stay in power.

• The influx of food aid can lower prices, making it harder for local small farmers to earn their livelihoods.

• Food aid can allow elite-controlled governments to continue avoiding the redistributive changes necessary to increase local production of food.

• Food aid distributed through food-for-work programs in fact benefits rural elites to the detriment of the rural poor. Such projects often improve the land of the elites and provide them with additional patronage possi-

bilities, while at best providing low-paid work during the slack season to the poor.

In our response to Question 16 we offered some conditions under which food aid might be helpful in an emergency. Certainly the 1979-1980 famine in Cambodia is an economically and politically created famine in which Americans have a responsibility to help alleviate the tremendous suffering of virtually an entire population. In such rare instances, however, it is probably the voluntary agencies who have a better chance of effectively mobilizing and distributing food aid.

Other than to meet such famine emergencies, the United States should announce a date for the termination of food aid to all countries where a narrowly based elite controls the economic system. This would most definitely include the largest recipients of U.S. food aid, such as Bangladesh, India, Indonesia, Pakistan and South Korea. Even a 1976 U.S. Senate study mission to Bangladesh concluded that food aid should be phased out over a five-year period.[1]

Concerned Americans should not think of food aid as *the* way to help the hungry. Dwelling on food aid—how much and what criteria should be used—diverts attention from the *process* of how hunger is created. It allows us to forget that the overriding impact of the United States on the ability of people to become food self-reliant is not through food aid but through the corporate, military, economic and covert involvement of the United States in their countries. We are thus advocating not only an end to chronic food aid but an end to all forms of government aid to countries where there is not already under way a fundamental democratization of control over productive resources.

18

In advocating a cutoff of official aid to so many countries, aren't you promoting a very cruel and chancy proposition: that even though an aid cutoff might hurt some people today, it is necessary so that structural changes can, in the longer run, eradicate hunger? After all, aren't there some good aid projects? Why not seek out the few successful projects and try to multiply them?

RESPONSE To let hunger increase while working for structural changes that in the future can address the underlying problems is *not* what we are saying.

The first question assumes that government aid at least lessens hunger, even if not addressing root causes. We are saying, however, that the overwhelming bulk of official aid projects do not alleviate hunger, directly or indirectly. As we have shown, they are more likely to increase hunger. To keep official aid flowing to elite, repressive regimes on the grounds that an undetermined but small portion of it actually does alleviate some hunger is to ignore and therefore maintain the overriding government-support functions of official aid. Such aid actually increases hunger and repression by reinforcing the power of national and international elites who usurp the resources rightfully belonging to the hungry. As the question suggests, official aid to narrowly based regimes does not simply fail to address root causes. It makes the addressing of root causes more difficult and therefore more distant.

The iceberg

When many Americans hear the word "aid," immediately they imagine a "project" somewhere in Africa or Latin America where a child who was starving yesterday is now eating. The Institute's work on foreign assistance tries to balance this gut-level impulse with knowledge not only of the concrete consequences of aid projects but, even more importantly, of *the overall impact of aid*. This book, therefore, focuses on the iceberg (not just on its tip)—on the general budgetary support that foreign aid provides to strategically positioned foreign governments, on its support for third world business interests and other urban elites, and on the support that foreign aid provides to a relatively few corporations in our own country. A few showcase projects can distract our attention from these overriding functions of government aid.

Question 18 is, probably, the one we are most frequently asked. Our response may sometimes be perceived as extreme. But even a recent director of AID, John Gilligan, endorsed a position that could lend support to our call for a halt to most current U.S. official aid. He approved this policy statement in 1979: "...should studies show that particular types of assistance, such as provision of current inputs, are exacerbating the plight of the poor in situations where land tenure practices are inequitable and there is an absence of commitment to reform, then the Agency, on Mission advice, is prepared to consider withholding those types of assistance."[1]

Our position may appear extreme because we see the issue of U.S. foreign assistance as one in which there is no conscionable middle ground: one either supports U.S. foreign aid to governments selected by our government and lives with the consequences we have detailed throughout our book (which we cannot do), or one works to halt U.S. economic and military assistance to all countries where a genuine redistribution of control over productive resources is not under way. While today there may be very few countries in this category, tomorrow there may be many more. That day might be sooner, we should keep in mind, if not for the U.S. government's support of third world governments which actively resist their own people's struggle for justice. U.S. support,

---

...official aid to narrowly based regimes...makes the addressing of root causes more difficult...

---

as we detail below, is much more extensive than just economic assistance.

Successful projects?

No doubt there *are* some successes — poor people in some countries who have been helped by U.S.-sponsored aid projects. We have learned, however, that it is not enough to be relieved that a few people have been helped, and to feel that our responsibility ends there. We must even question the meaning of these "successes." Some questions we ask when we learn of a situation in which aid has apparently helped some poor people are these:

1. *Who* are the beneficiaries?

Are they part of that country's dispossessed — the growing numbers of people with little or no access to land and without prospect for work? Or are the beneficiaries part of a poor but more advantaged strata with access to sufficient resources to use the aid-financed inputs profitably?

2. How does the success of the project's beneficiaries affect the chances for progress by the majority of people?

If, for example, the relative handful of people within the project have doubled their income, what will their relationship be to their neighbors who have not prospered? Will the newly advantaged now identify with the status quo and stand with local and international interests to oppose redistribution in control over resources? If so, the tragic result of a "successful" aid project might be to thwart efforts by the poor to unite and thereby resist the system that now robs them of power and dignity.

3. Can the project's success be multiplied on a broader scale, given resource constraints? Or is the project just an artificial showcase? Often the per capita investment in a foreign aid-sponsored project is so great that it is completely unfeasible on a national scale. A World Bank resettlement scheme in Malaysia, for example, cost over $13,000 per family![2] (And there are many more such examples.)

Additional questions that should be raised in evaluating any development project are suggested in our response to Question 19.

We are not saying that direct material help to the poor abroad is completely impossible. But if there is a chance that outside resources will help rather than hurt, it is through voluntary, nongovernmental aid agencies (as we discuss in Question 19), not through official aid. Even then, achieving positive results from aid is far from certain. What results will depend on how many questions, which we raise in response to Question 19, are answered.

Removing the obstacles

We sense that the very preoccupation with increasing or improving our foreign aid means that few Americans understand that aid is only *one,* and not even the largest, channel through which the U.S. government affects the forces that maintain hunger and underdevelopment abroad. Few realize that the U.S. government, through more than a dozen channels, gives economic and military assistance to regimes that it identifies as serving its interest.[3] None of these channels are considered part of our foreign assistance. Yet their impact on the lives of the vast majority of people in the third world is both more sweeping and profound.

Probably more than through aid or direct coup d'etat interventions—such as Iran (1953), Guatemala (1954), the Dominican Republic (1965) and Cambodia (1970)—the U.S. government influences what goes on in numer-

Rice threshing machine, International Rice Research Institute, Los Banos, the Philippines. The World Bank loans money for research at the Institute. The mechanical threshing machine displaces many workers.

ous countries by propping up regimes through non-aid economic channels and through military assistance and sales. The U.S. government invariably uses such power to support economic and political "stability." In many countries "stability" means maintaining a situation in which the majority are deprived of basic human needs and rights. For this reason, U.S. influence in many cases is opposed to the well-being of the poor majority.

These multiple channels of economic and military influence are neither dramatic nor obvious. Indeed, it is their lack of drama that makes these channels so invisible.

These multiple channels of influence serve as day-to-day supports for the forces of concentrated wealth and power abroad that help create the day-to-day suffering of the poor majority. It is these often invisible channels about which we must become more knowledgeable. How many Americans, for example, have ever heard of the International Monetary Fund,† the Export-Import Bank,† the Commodity Credit Corporation,† or the Overseas Private Investment Corporation?†

International Monetary Fund

The International Monetary

---

† See "A Primer: Some Essential Facts about the Aid Establishment" at the end of this book for an in-depth description.

Fund (IMF) was established by the United States and the major Western European nations at the close of World War II. With a current membership of 140 countries, the IMF's official purpose is to promote international monetary cooperation, and the expansion of international trade and monetary convertibility and stability.[4]

Michael Moffitt of the Institute for Policy Studies notes that the IMF has little power over the economies of the industrial countries. He identifies the IMF's major role as lender of the last resort for third world governments who are deeply in debt to private international banks.[5] In this role, the IMF exerts considerable power over third world economies and operates in the interests of private international banks.

Since 1973, according to Moffitt, the IMF has been promoting international deflation as the solution to global monetary imbalances. But since the IMF has little influence over the policies of the industrial countries, it has mainly promoted deflation in the third world countries. Its main lever to compel third world countries to reduce their external deficits (at least temporarily) is the "conditionality" it attaches to loans that it offers when a country has exceeded its official quota and still needs assistance.

This lever of "conditionality" in loans to third world governments works in part because in addition to the sizable financial resources the IMF controls (by 1979, $45 billion in national quota subscriptions), it has the power to create international money in the form of Special Drawing Rights (SDRs).

Upon joining the IMF, a member country is allotted a certain quota of SDRs—a non-traded reserve currency used only for accounting purposes—based on its "economic strength." When a country needs foreign exchange to finance balance of payments deficits, it can borrow SDRs in exchange for its own currency, and repay the loan within a certain specified period. As long as a member country borrows only up to the equivalent of its quota, there is no "conditionality," that is, no imposition by the IMF of economic policies on the borrowing country.

Once a member has exhausted its quota, however, it must accept economic policy conditions set by the IMF. For example, to borrow an additional 25 percent of its quota, a country must produce an IMF-approved "financial stabilization" program, including fiscal, exchange rate, and trade policies to improve its payments deficit position over the duration of a loan (usually one year). But not until a country borrows the equivalent of 75 percent above its quota does the IMF, under the special "standby credit arrangement," begin to demand strict adherence to economic "stabilization" policies. Certain performance criteria must be met by a country before each installment of the loan is approved. Moreover, strict control over government finance—revenues, expenditures, taxes, subsidies, debt ceilings and so forth—is stipulated.[6]

Once a country has borrowed the equivalent of double its quota and still needs help, it turns to the "Extended Fund Facility" of the IMF. From this point on, the IMF will exert almost complete control over a country's internal economic policies for the normal three-year duration of the program. Currently, five countries are under Extended Fund Facility arrangements with the IMF: Egypt, Haiti, Jamaica, Sri Lanka, and the Philippines.

Without approval from the IMF, a third world government has great difficulty obtaining loans from either private banks, multilateral development banks, or other governments.[7]

In most cases, a country negotiating a stand-by agreement with the IMF is obliged to:

• Devalue its currency to boost exports and limit imports. If much food is imported, the result is higher food prices.

• Cut government spending. The first cuts are health, housing and education programs designed for the poor.

• Introduce wage controls, undercutting the already marginal income of the poor without concomitant price controls on basic necessities.

• Raise interest rates, making it more difficult for farmers and small businesses to get credit. The result can be more unemployment and less food production.

• Remove barriers to foreign investment and free trade. Free trade means that luxury items may still be imported even when scarce foreign exchange should be used to bring in basic items. An open door to foreign investment allows foreign corporations to get a foothold in the economy at bargain rates, at a time when land prices and wages are kept low by all of the above policies.

While the direct effects of IMF stabilization programs on the poor majority have often been documented in terms of falling real wages and rising malnutrition, no legislation has passed the U.S. Congress which in any way directs the U.S. executive director of the IMF to take minimal human needs or other human rights into consideration in formulating economic programs. During 1978, attempts to attach amendments to legislation authorizing funds for the IMF's new supplemental financing facility (the Witteveen Facility) were all unsuccessful.

The imposition of IMF policy guidelines, resulting in dramatic price rises for basic necessities without corresponding wage increases, has set off riots in Peru, Turkey and Egypt. When Egypt was forced to end food subsidies and reduce fuel and clothing subsidies to meet IMF stipulations in 1977, people unable to afford these necessities rioted; 78 people were killed.[8]

Peru's experience with the IMF is revealing. Between 1975 and 1977, the World Bank and private banks encouraged Peru to incur a multibillion dollar debt. Eager to get rid of their Arab oil money glut, bankers were betting on an oil boom in Peru and high prices for Peru's copper. Instead, the oil boom dwindled to a trickle and prices fell for Peru's export commodities. On top of this, Peru's anchovy crop, a major source of foreign exchange, virtually disappeared.

In 1976, the IMF stepped in to "rescue the nation" from bankruptcy. In 1979, a Roman Catholic priest in Peru wrote a searing critique of the impact of IMF policies which have cut worker buying power in half. In addition, the price of bread has jumped 1,000 percent and infant mortality has climbed 30 percent, an increase of 13,000 infant deaths per year. "The social costs of the [IMF] program have been awful," he concluded.[9]

The IMF has also been criticized on the grounds that its loan approvals reflect the biases of its most powerful members. In 1977, the right-wing government in Argentina was granted a $194 million loan without having to control one of the highest inflation rates in Latin America. During the same period, Peru and Jamaica were forced to meet rigid inflaton control criteria. In Jamaica, where a democratic government is working toward agrarian reform and more local control of natural resources, food prices shot up 40 percent in less than a year due to IMF-imposed policies.[10]

In 1977, the IMF loaned $465 million to the apartheid South African government to cover a deficit caused by increased spending for police and the military. While publicly espousing an anti-apartheid policy, the Carter administration gave approval for the loan.[11]

In late 1979, the IMF claimed to have relaxed its rules governing "conditionality." The IMF said that it would "pay due regard to the domestic and social and political objectives" of borrowers. That third world countries would prefer to borrow from private banks is an indication that they still see the IMF in the role of dictating social policies.[12]

While formally controlled by a board of governors on which each member government is represented, the decisionmaking power within the IMF resides with the 21 executive directors. Five of the executive directors are appointed by the five members with the largest quota—the United States, the United Kingdom, West Germany, France and Japan. The United States holds approximately 21 percent of the voting power. The remaining 16 executive directors are elected by the other 135 member countries.[13] Although the IMF appears to be an international body, Americans have a special responsibility for the impact of its policies due to the power the United States exerts within it.

Export-Import Bank

Eximbank, as it is commonly known, is an independent U.S. federal agency authorized to make loans and issue loan guarantees and insurance to foreign governments and businesses for purchase of U.S. manufactured goods. While not officially designated as an aid agency, the Eximbank directly aids private business enterprises in other countries by providing low-interest credit to purchasers of U.S. products. In FY 1978, the flow of Eximbank loans to the third world, about $3.75 billion, easily doubled the volume of project aid extended by AID.[14] In fact, the Eximbank is the largest source of U.S. support for 32 third world countries.[15]

As a result of lobbying by powerful U.S. corporations and the Carter administration, Eximbank's direct loan activities increased fivefold between fiscal years 1977 and 1979—from $700 million to $3.75 billion. President Carter has asked Congress to authorize $4.1 billion in Eximbank credits for fiscal year 1980.[16]

The Eximbank provides loans to whatever countries it chooses, and on the terms and for what kind of businesses it chooses. (Human rights advocates have attempted to amend Eximbank's authorizing legislation to prohibit loans to South Africa. Despite these efforts, Eximbank loans, guarantees and insurance to the South Africa apartheid regime exceeded $32 million in 1978 FY.[17]) In the six-month period ending in March 1978, the Eximbank channeled $210 million in loans and insurance to 11 nations classified by the Department of State as serious violators of human rights, including Iran under the Shah, the Philippines, Nicaragua under Somoza, South Korea and Taiwan.[18] During the first four years following the imposition of martial law in 1972, Eximbank lending to the Philippines increased over 300 percent.[19]

Between 1970 and 1978, almost two-thirds of the activities of the Eximbank went to support commercial trade with third world countries. The bulk of these loans went to so-called middle-income developing countries, such as Brazil, South Korea and Mexico.[20]

Nuclear power is first on the list of commercial activities suggested by the Eximbank, accounting for 19 percent of the total Eximbank budget of $26 billion.[21] Eximbank, with a commitment of over $6 billion in loans and loan guarantees, has financed 47 of the 59 nuclear plants exported by U.S. companies.[22] Aircraft and transportation, mining and refining equipment are other major items funded by the Eximbank.

The largest corporate beneficiaries of Eximbank operations to date—each having received more than $.5 billion in credit authorization—are Boeing, Westinghouse, General Electric, McDonnell Douglas, Caterpillar, General Motors, Allis-Chalmers and Chrysler.[23]

Unlike AID, the Eximbank does not have to go to Congress for annual appropriations. The Bank's initial capitalization by the Treasury Department was $1 billion and it raises additional funds in private credit markets with a Treasury Department guarantee. Because it holds a U.S. Treasury guarantee, the Eximbank is able to borrow at low interest rates and thus can re-lend at less than market rates.

The Eximbank is governed by a board appointed by the President. Semi-weekly board meetings are ostensibly open to public scrutiny. Exemption from the "Government in the Sunshine Act," however, allows Eximbank proceedings to occur privately to avoid disclosure of "trade secrets and commercial or financial information obtained from a person and privileged or confidential."[24]

Commodity Credit Corporation

The Commodity Credit Corporation (CCC) offers medium and short-term credit below commercial rates to foreign purchasers of U.S. agricultural commodities. In 1978, the CCC financed $1.6 billion in agricultural

exports from the United States.

Despite its defined purpose to serve as a mechanism for expanding export markets, CCC programs also provide the U.S. government with a mechanism for supporting selected foreign governments. A recent analysis of CCC programs by the Comptroller General's office noted that "Recipient countries receive substantial economic benefits in the form of domestic budget and balance-of-payment support."[25] In 1978, according to the report, the CCC approved a three-year, $170 million credit for the South Korean government to purchase wheat and feed grains. It was later learned that the Korean government resold the imported grain on repayment terms of 90 days or less. The report cites a similar resale of wheat financed by CCC loans in the Philippines. Although there were "no appar-

Produce vendors enroute to market in Cox's Bazaar, Bangladesh.

ent irregularities" in the Philippines, the Comptroller General's report noted that "the Philippine government, not the millers and general population, was the beneficiary of the CCC credit."[26]

Overseas Private Investment Corporation (OPIC)

OPIC, an insurance program backed by the U.S. Treasury Department, guarantees corporate investment abroad against losses incurred when a local currency cannot be converted into U.S. dollars, and against war damage or expropriation. Through OPIC, the Treasury Department backed foreign private investments totaling almost $9 billion in 1978.[27]

Originally established in 1950 to encourage U.S. business investments in post-war Europe, OPIC has evolved into a program to assist the expansion of U.S. multinational corporations into third world countries. In an amendment to the Foreign Assistance Act in 1971, OPIC was mandated "to mobilize and facilitate the participation of United States private capital and skills in the economic and social progress of less developed friendly countries and areas, thereby complementing the development assistance objectives of the United States."[28]

OPIC also makes *direct loans* to U.S. companies for investments in third world countries, shares the cost of some pre-investment surveys, and organizes "missions" of potential corporate investors to select countries.

Nearly two-thirds of all U.S. corporate investment (excluding petroleum) in underdeveloped countries is insured by OPIC.[29] The principal beneficiaries of OPIC are among the largest multinational corporations. In 1978, 68 percent of all OPIC insurance went to companies on *Fortune* magazine's listing of the 1,000 largest U.S. companies. **A mere 10 corporations received over one-half of the total investment insurance issued by OPIC during 1978.**[30] These top 10 include Chase Manhattan, International Paper, Manufacturer's Hanover Trust, Hooker Chemical and General Electric. OPIC has insured Del Monte's pineapple processing plant in Kenya and Ralston Purina's fast food chains in Brazil. In 1978, the Chase Manhattan Bank in Vietnam, the Bank of America in Chile, and Revere Copper and Brass in Jamaica were the beneficiaries of settlement claims for investment losses.[30]

OPIC's activities are also highly concentrated geographically. Approximately two-thirds of OPIC's activity is in only six countries: Brazil, the Philippines, South Korea, Indonesia, Taiwan and the Dominican Republic; all are countries with notably repressive governments.[32]

OPIC is not simply a passive agent; it helps seek investment opportunities. It describes its own role as "brokerage": seeking the most promising investments and making a "concerted effort to interest American companies in them."[33] In agriculture, according to OPIC official Pat Counts, "our OPIC policy...limits our assistance to projects involving large land holdings."[34]

All of OPIC's obligations are backed by the U.S. Treasury Department. This liability of the Treasury Department, which may easily be for several hundred million dollars in a single country, can affect U.S. policy toward a particular foreign government. For instance, in testifying before the Senate on the CIA's intervention in the presidential elections in Chile, former U.S. ambassador to Chile Edward Korry noted the potential cost to the Treasury Department of covering investment guarantees in case of legal expropriation.[35]

In 1978, due to opposition in Congress, OPIC almost failed to obtain renewal of its authority. Opposition was based largely on organized labor's claim that OPIC support of multinational corporations facilitated the relocation of manufacturing plants to low-wage labor sites outside the United States. Some opposition was also based on the conviction that OPIC hinders the development of a pro-democratic foreign policy.

When authorized channels for U.S. aid are closed, as when Congress cut off formal aid to the junta in Chile, commercial links are simply redirected through hidden doors such as OPIC. While our formal economic aid program to the military government in Brazil has dwindled to a few million dollars worth of food aid, the Eximbank and OPIC together provided loans, loan guarantees, and insurance worth almost half a billion dollars in FY 1977 to the commercial interests which finance Brazil's extremely repressive dictatorship.[36]

U.S. military assistance and sales

We must also weigh the impact of the powerful and overriding influence of our military assistance and sales programs as well as foreign covert operations (the CIA*) that maintain the status quo abroad. The status quo in most countries is widespread hunger.

In violation of foreign aid legislation explicitly prohibiting military assistance and sales to "gross violators of internationally recognized human rights," such assistance and arms sales continued in fiscal year 1980 to at least nine regimes that have been widely denouced for their violation of human rights. They are Zaire, Paraguay, Indonesia, the Philippines, Guatemala, Thai-

---

* Only a few high officials and virtually no taxpayers know how much is spent by the CIA in its covert operations in third world countries. The House Select Committee on Intelligence, however, did identify the four major areas of these operations. One-third of the CIA's funds are spent to influence or subvert democratic elections. Another one-third manipulates the mass media—planting propaganda, etc. The rest is divided between penetrating independent associations with "agents of influence" and directly exporting the means of violence: paramilitary operations, mercenaries, arms and ammunition.[37]

land, Bangladesh, El Salvador and South Korea.[38]

U.S. military support for foreign governments comes in a variety of forms: grants and credits for arms, equipment and services; deliveries of "surplus" weapons; and training and education for foreign military personnel.

Military Assistance Program (MAP). The MAP grants arms, equipment and services to foreign governments. Military assistance amounts to four times that of development project aid to the third world, excluding the Middle East.[39] Under this program the United States provided over $53 billion worth of free military supplies from 1950 to 1979.[40] Well over $30 billion of this has gone to third world nations outside the Middle East.

Excess Defense Articles (EDA). Through the EDA program, the Department of Defense grants "surplus" arms and equipment to foreign governments. From 1950 through 1979, the U.S. government gave $6.4 billion worth of "surplus" military hardware to at least 60 nations, mostly in the third world.[41] The actual value is doubtlessly much higher. Moreover, while the dollar value might seem low (by U.S. government standards!), it should be noted that EDA grants often go to smaller, low-income countries. For instance, during the period cited, over $11 million

Teff harvest, Ethiopia. The IDA and SIDA financed a road project through this region.

in EDA has gone to the notoriously repressive military dictatorship of General Stroessner in Paraguay.[42]

In 1976, Congress tried to control the U.S. military role in the third world by limiting the number of military advisors that could be permanently stationed abroad. The effect has been negligible. By the time Congress passed the legislation, most U.S.-supported advisory, training and technical assistance was supplied by roving armed forces personnel (thus sidestepping the congressional limitations on permanent stationing) and by civilians —11,320 employees of the 50 U.S. arms manufacturers. In the era of highly sophisticated military hardware, technicians employed by U.S. Department of Defense contractors are selling these arms, and are a major part of the U.S. military presence in the third world.[43]

At the heart of the new U.S. military presence abroad are Mobile Training Teams (MTTs) and Technical Assistance Field Teams (TAFTs). Team members, wearing civilian clothes despite their military status, enter a country unobtrusively as advisors, trainers and maintenance specialists.

In addition to MTTs and TAFTs, U.S. military advisors are permanently stationed in countries such as Argentina, Brazil, Chile, El Salvador, Uruguay and the Philippines, on whom military aid sanctions have been placed by Congress for human rights violations.[44]

Foreign Military Sales (FMS). FMS is a program of sales arrangement and credit for foreign government purchases of arms. The FMS program covers all sales which are arranged through the Department of Defense, although not all such sales receive U.S. government financing. From 1955 through 1979, sales were over $97 billion.[45] FMS sales have rapidly expanded in recent years, reaching $13 billion in fiscal year 1979, as the U.S. government has promoted military sales to partly offset rising trade deficits.[46]

Many items sold under the FMS program are also used domestically. Such FMS items include but are not limited to barbed wire, armored cars and tear gas grenades. For instance, under the FMS program the Shah of Iran obtained 350,000 gas masks and 11,500 tear gas grenades.[47]

Through FMS and a growing commercial sales effort (including the government's Commercial Sales Program), the United States stands as the number one arms merchant in the world. The United States supplied 52 percent of the total arms transferred to the third world from 1967 to 1976. Arms sales by U.S. corporations to foreign countries in the period from 1971 to 1979 amounted to $8.3 billion.[48] FMS program sales to third world governments expanded over twentyfold in the 1970s, from $500 million in 1970 to $10 billion in 1978, and now account for 81 percent of U.S. arms sales worldwide.[49] Worldwide, three-quarters of transfers in armaments are to third world nations.

From 1955 to 1979, the U.S. government extended $19.9 billion in FMS credits to 53 countries, mostly in the third world.[50] In fiscal year 1979, FMS credits covered $5.7 billion of the $13 billion of U.S. military sales to the third world; the rest were "hard cash" sales.[51]

Foreign Military Training. The International Military Education and Training Program (IMET) and the Military Assistance Program (MAP) provide training for foreign military personnel in the United States, the Panama Canal Zone, and at a number of other locations around the world. From 1950 to 1979, these two programs trained 495,000 foreign military officers and students from 80 countries. The IMET cost (excluding the MAP portion) to U.S. taxpayers was $1.95 billion. In fiscal year 1979, the IMET program cost $28.1 million and enrolled military personnel from 41 countries, 36 of which are third world nations.[52]

Foreign Police Training. Since 1961, the United States has operated several programs to train domestic police forces from third world countries. The principal program, AID's Public Safety Program, dispensed over $200 million worth of arms and equipment to foreign police organizations, trained over 7,500 officers at special schools in the United States, and provided basic training to over one million policemen at U.S.-sponsored police academies abroad.[53]

The *Public Safety Program* was disbanded in 1975 by an act of Congress which prohibited the use of public funds to provide arms, equipment and other support for police forces abroad. Since 1975, the Department of State's International Narcotics Control program (INC) has distributed over $200 million worth of arms, equipment and training to many of the same police units previously supported by the Public Safety Program. There is considerable evidence that such equipment and trained personnel, while theoretically restricted to anti-drug programs, are used in non-drug activities as well, including counter-insurgency operations in the countryside.[54] Major recipients include Mexico, Thailand and Colombia. The INC program, as did the Public Safety Program on which it was modeled, consists of grants of equipment and training to foreign policy forces.

Police Arms Sales. The Office of Munitions Control within the Department of State authorizes sales by private U.S. arms merchants to foreign police forces. These sales are estimated at $200 million annually.[55] Between 1973 and 1976, the top U.S. armaments companies sold to foreign governments the following police equipment: 50,000 pistols and revolvers; 10,000 submachine guns; 155,000 tear gas grenades; and 6,600 canisters of chemical mace.[56]

Moreover, much of the arms, training and equipment provided

under MAP, EDA and IMET programs is used for internal police operations, despite the 1975 congressional prohibition on aid to foreign police forces.[57] In many third world countries, especially those under martial law, the military functions as a domestic police apparatus.[58] In Nicaragua, until his popular overthrow in July 1979, dictator Somoza was kept in power by the brutal National Guard, operating as both an army and a policing force. The National Guard was provided more U.S. training than any other military or police force in the western hemisphere on a per capita basis.[59] The Philippines Constabulary (PC)—another military-style police force recruited and trained through the armed forces—benefits directly from U.S. support to the Philippine armed forces. The PC and the armed forces rotate personnel and share facilities. The PC uses the regular army's logistics center supplied by the U.S. Military Assistance Program.[60]

CHART IV

Ten Top Recipients Get Three-Quarters of Allocated U.S. Food Aid ($ millions, proposed, FY 1980)

1.	Egypt	**219.6**
2.	India	**110.5**
3.	Indonesia	**107.5**
4.	Bangladesh	**78.0**
5.	Pakistan	**41.5**
6.	Portugal	**40.0**
7.	South Korea	**40.0**
8.	Peru	**31.3**
9.	Haiti	**27.7**
10.	Sri Lanka	**26.1**

Ten Top Recipients: **$722.2**

All 66 Other Recipients: **$252.8**

Total Allocated Food Aid: **$975.0**

Source: AID Congressional Presentation Fiscal Year 1980, p. 128.

One way of removing the obstacles to change in underdeveloped countries is to expose and work to end such props supplied by the U.S. government to repressive regimes abroad. It is equally important to remove obstacles where a government is genuinely attempting reform and greater participation. A case in point is Nicaragua in 1980. The new government's efforts to begin building a new society are thwarted by enormous debts incurred under the Somoza dictatorship. With much of the debt due for repayment, the new government is gravely pressured to rebuild the Somoza-like, export-oriented economy rather than building a new economy where people produce first for their own basic needs. Yet, the U.S. government prefers to offer aid, in the form of *more loans,* for projects that it can oversee. The programs would largely benefit Nicaraguan and U.S. corporations. U.S. policymakers want to maintain their influence so that the new society will not formulate policies that would threaten U.S. corporate interests. Exposing and opposing such manipulations is a responsibility of all of us who want to ally ourselves with the self-determination of the poor majority in Nicaragua.

Our responsibility

The question seems to assume that without U.S. intervention in the form of better "projects" there is little hope for progress by the poor; it assumes that official government aid is our most direct link to the needlessly hungry abroad. Neither, we believe, is true.

In every country where people are suffering, there is already movement for change. People do not suffer willingly. In some countries, like the Philippines, the grass roots resistance and drive for greater justice is increasingly well organized; in others, like Haiti, it is just beginning. Yet in all cases, our prime responsibility is to work to end support for the enemies of the poor and hungry—beginning by exposing the uses and impact of *all types* of government economic and military aid. This is *not* folding one's hands in defeat or despair. It is a powerful contribution.

19

QUESTION

You have talked only about official, government-to-government aid. What about "voluntary," nongovernmental organizations? Is nongovernmental aid the solution?

RESPONSE The Institute's field and desk research on aid has focused on official government aid from the United States. With limited financial resources we simply have had to make a choice. In the future we hope to investigate the work of some of the voluntary agencies we are most asked about. Although unable to carry out our own systematic investigation thus far, the Institute is fortunate to be part of an international network committed to sharing the information gained firsthand on the impact of voluntary aid efforts. We regularly receive letters and informal reports from people around the world. And, of course, in our field work in various countries we learn, albeit unsystematically, of various voluntary aid projects. In all of this, most impressive is the difficulty that even the best voluntary agencies appear to have in their attempts to avoid the dynamic we find endemic to official aid—the reinforcement of oppressive, elite-controlled economic and political structures.

Theoretically, voluntary agencies have several advantages over official aid agencies.

First they need not work *through* the local government. In the few countries allowing freedom of association and speech, they can work openly with and through legal organizations. In most countries, however, where the government infiltrates or brutally represses movements for change, they must work very discreetly if they are to directly support indigenous efforts that are building alternatives. (Later we share with you an example from Bangladesh.) Often such indigenous efforts are within religious organizations or in the form of liberation movements.

Nonetheless, the majority of voluntary agencies, especially the largest, seem to opt to collaborate directly with foreign governments, including some of the world's most repressive ones. There are even cases where U.S. official aid has been cut off because of government repression and oppression only to have a major U.S. voluntary agency step in to help finance that same government's programs. In Chile, for example, Catholic Relief Services (CRS) is collaborating with the Pinochet military government in a large food donation program. The program is part and parcel of economic policies that have generated increased poverty and hunger in Chile. Even the Catholic cardinal has told CRS that the program is "seriously injurious" and that, because of CRS's collaboration, "the image of the Catholic church in the face of the poor is being discolored." The CRS collaboration originally set for one year has been extended three times.[1]

A second potential advantage for voluntary agencies is that their programs need not reflect the strategic and corporate interests dominating the U.S. government. Unfortunately, many of the private voluntary organizations (PVOs)† have become heavily dependent on U.S. government monies, making them increasingly indistinguishable from agents of the U.S. government. This disturbing possibility was strengthened by 1974 "New Directions" foreign aid legislation which established an office within AID to award grants for overseas programs of voluntary organizations. (It was very troubling for us to learn that a major church feels it cannot help financially support our Institute's investigations into the impact of U.S. government aid because its "overseas aid program depends on money from AID.")

Still, there are voluntary aid organizations such as Oxfam-America, World Neighbors, and the Mennonite Central Committee that strictly refuse U.S. government funds.

A third advantage is that voluntary agencies can work in countries from which the U.S. government is expressly withholding official aid—countries like Mozambique, Vietnam, Laos and Cuba (where the governments are part of the redistribution of benefits from resources). Those few American voluntary agencies that thus far have chosen to work in these countries tell us that they, like a number of European and Canadian government aid programs, opt to do so precisely because such are among the few countries where the government is not working *against* broad-based development.

A fourth advantage is that voluntary aid organizations are more likely to have the willingness and capability to finance projects requiring small sums of money. This contrasts sharply with AID and the multilateral development banks where, if anything, the trend is to insist upon large-dollar projects to minimize paper work. Many development workers, including frustrated ones within AID, have stressed to us that in those rare cases where outside material support can be useful, it is invariably a small sum of money that is needed. In fact, they tell us, larger sums can be destructive. Of course, some voluntary agencies, especially the larger ones, might well have bu-

---

† See "A Primer: Some Essential Facts about the Aid Establishment" for an in-depth description.

reaucratic imperatives similar to those of AID. Some voluntary agency workers, seeing only the need for small sums (to free, say, a local person for a few hours of catalytic organizing work among her or his own people) are told by their headquarters that unless larger sums are given, the donors back home will conclude too great a portion of the overall budget goes for "administration."

Since we are not now able to provide assessments of individual voluntary aid organizations and their myriad of projects (an impossible task!), we decided to share with you some basic questions we would urge you to ask about any development project to which you or your organization is considering giving support:

Ten Questions to Ask about a Development Project

1. Whose project is it? Is it the donor agency's
   or
   Does it originate with the people involved?

2. Does the project define the problem to be tackled as a technical or physical deficiency (e.g., poor farming methods or depleted soils) that can be overcome with the right technique and skills?
   or
   Does it first address the underlying social, economic and political constraints that stand in the way of solving the physical or technical problem?

3. Does the project strengthen the economic and political position of a certain group, creating a more prosperous enclave which then becomes resistant to change that might abolish its privileges?
   or
   Does it generate a shift in power to the powerless?

4. Does the project focus only on the needs of individuals?
   or
   Does it help individuals who are now powerless to see their common interest with others who are also exploited, thus leading to unified efforts through which collective strength is built?

5. Does the project merely help individuals adjust to their exploitation by such external forces as the national government or the international market?
   or
   Does it encourage an understanding of that exploitation and a resistance to it?

6. Do new skills and information remain only with the leaders?
   or
   Does the project involve an ongoing educational process for all the participants?

7. Does the project, through the intervention of outside experts, take away local initiative?
   or
   Does it generate a process of democratic decisionmaking and a thrust toward self-reli-

ance that can carry over to future projects?

8. Does the project reinforce dependence on outside sources for material and skills?

or

Does it call forth local ingenuity, local labor and local materials, and can it be maintained with local skills?

9. Will success only be measured by the achievement of objectives specified at the outset?

or

Is the project open-ended, with success measured as the project progresses?

10. Is the evaluation a one-way process by which the donor judges the recipient's performance?

or

Is it a two-way (if possible face-to-face) dialogue in which the recipient also evaluates the donor and they together evaluate the project?

It would be naive to assume that any organization could score 100 percent in answer to these questions. The work of any development group undoubtedly will fall somewhere on a continuum. The first critical measure, however, is whether or not the outside development agency sees its role as going into another country "to set things right" or sees itself as a supporter of progressive indigenous forces already underway. In other words, does the outside group understand that in every country where people are hungry, something is *already* happening? Our role is not to start the train moving but to remove the obstacles in its way—especially those originating in our own country—and to provide fuel for the train, *if needed*.

What U.S.-based groups do we know that take this approach and are struggling with the difficult questions we have just posed? Certainly we are not capable of endorsing all the projects of any organization, but we can point to positive examples. It is up to all of us to learn more about such organizations and support what we find to be positive.

The Economic Development Bureau (EDB) is one such organization. While working in Tanzania's Ministry of Planning, American economist Idrian Resnick was struck by the Tanzanians' own capacity to do much of what they were asking foreigners to do.

In 1975, he established the EDB as a consulting service on development problems that would offer groups in the third world an alternative to the World Bank and AID "experts." The more than 300 EDB associates from over 35 countries have technical knowledge in varied areas but do not see the problem of development merely as a technical one. They understand that their knowledge can be constructive only after the local community has begun building a democratic and collective decisionmaking process.

The contrast between the EDB

Wheat harvest, Kahorole, Bangladesh.

approach and that of a typical consulting agency is most revealing.[2] In Tanzania, a country with one of the lowest nutritional levels in the world, 25 to 40 percent of the grain is lost each year due to mildew, vermin, and insect infestation. At the request of the Tanzanian government, the Swedish International Development Agency hired several consulting firms to examine the grain storage problem. In three years, the consultants produced four reports—all recommending highly mechanized, extremely expensive silos, and all requiring foreign technicians to run them. An additional $.75 million dollars was recommended for further designs by consultants! Six years after the first report, no silos had been built.

Enter the EDB. Invited by the Community Development Trust Fund of Tanzania, the EDB decided to attack the problem at the village level and in such a way as to ensure the direct control by the villagers throughout the project. The EDB team, including a Tanzanian trained in the learning theories of exiled Brazilian Paulo Freire, and others with knowledge of village storage alternatives, entered the village. The villagers formed a storage committee. The team initiated a discussion in which the participants worked together to gain an understanding of the forces preventing them from adequately handling and storing their grains. The problem was not simply a matter of rats, mildew and bugs, or of drying, spraying and rebuilding. Uncovering and understanding the social and economic relations in the village were necessary before effective action was possible.

First, as one of the EDB consultants put it, "It was necessary to convince the villagers that we did not have a preconceived idea... 'up our sleeve' all the time just waiting for the little drama of village democracy to play itself out.'' The credibility of the EDB technicians was established only when, in response to serious criticism by the villagers, they dropped a design that they had put forward in discussion. Only then did the villagers believe that they had not come "with an answer."

The villagers soon came to realize that a great deal of effective technology already existed right there. But because the village is composed of many ethnic groups, neighbors were often unaware of each other's structures and methods. Through sharing experiences, the people became conscious of the richness of their varied knowledge and experience. Rather than introducing a foreign technology, the successful storage system that evolved turned out to be a recombination of the best elements in the traditional storage methods of the village. The people were part of a dynamic unfolding of events rather than on the receiving end of a technical exercise.

Initially, the EDB was not totally satisfied with the results. The project did succeed in completing 20 rat-proof, elevated sorghum storage structures in one harvest season but this process did not immediately spread to other villages. Three years later, however, the EDB learned from a Tanzanian adult educator involved in the project that there is now widespread interest in it among Tanzanian development workers and that other regions in Tanzania intend to improve their grain storage facilities in a similar way. In EDB terms, the project is a success: the Tanzanians have integrated the approach into their own rural development plans, eliminating the need for outside consultants.

Building on the Tanzanian experience, the EDB undertook a second grain storage project in Guinea Bissau in 1979 and 1980, which was led by a woman adult educator. The project trained 12 Guinean teams and two counterparts in the techniques of mobilization through conscientization dialogue and the development of improved grain storage techniques based largely on village technology. The project covered six clusters of villages. The EDB team used socio-drama in the training process, and the project produced a manual which can be used by village-level workers from all ministeries, as well as school teachers, for duplicating the project or mobilizing peasants for changes other than grain storage improvement.

In Bangladesh, a country in which Americans have been made to see only passivity and hopelessness, at least three organizations founded and directed by Bangladeshis are tackling problems such as landlessness, the oppression of women, and the lack of credit and health care—the most difficult problems facing people in the countryside. One organization, Gono Unnayan Prochesta, is supported by the American Friends

Service Committee. Another is Gonoshasthaya Kendra, supported by a number of progressive foreign groups including Inter Pares (Canadian) and Terre des Hommes (Holland and Switzerland).[3]

Gonoshasthaya Kendra's work includes such village-based programs as agricultural loans to sharecroppers to help them become independent of their landlords and local usurious creditors, a health insurance program based on village paramedics, and the training of women to fill the great need for carpenters, blacksmiths and plumbers, jobs traditionally performed only by men.

Such groups have no illusions

Simulia many times.''

A third example in Bangladesh is the Bangladesh Rural Advancement Committee (BRAC), supported by Oxfam-America.[4] BRAC's projects focus on functional education for Bangladesh's poorest groups, which means literacy achieved through discussion that focuses on "real life problems." Literacy and, therefore, the chance for a basic education are seen by BRAC as tools for the poor villagers to grasp the forces limiting their lives, and as a first step for the poor in taking action against those forces.

Functional education lays the basis, then, of BRAC's action

. . . the successful storage system that evolved turned out to be a recombination of the best elements in the traditional storage methods. . .

about the difficulty of their work and the risks involved. In 1976, one of the paramedics was killed by a local doctor who felt his business was threatened. The murderers, known by the police, still roam free. But the obvious risk is paralleled by the equally obvious bravery of the villagers. On the anniversary of his death, all the paramedics organized a five-mile walk to the site of the murder. One participant wrote, "Along the way, about 300 villagers spontaneously joined the procession; they had known Nizam [the victim] well who had walked and cycled the path to

thrust. In forming cooperatives, such groups as the landless, women, and exploited fisherpeople gain strength through pulling together resources and working toward common goals. One example is BRAC's work with a landless group in the village of Atgaon.[5]

Atgaon, a village of about 2,000 in northeast Bangladesh, is fairly typical: two percent are rich landowners (with 40 to 50 acres) while 30 percent are very small farmers (with two to seven acres). Fully 40 percent of the villagers are landless and very poor.

At stake in the village (particularly for the landless) was control of the "khas" land—mostly land confiscated from those who abandoned the country after the 1971 war of liberation from Pakistan. In theory, khas land—reportedly 10 percent of all cultivated land in the country—belongs to the government and any landless cultivator can apply for permanent rights. In fact, however, large landholders control much of the khas land, typically using it for grazing but sometimes for cultivation.

In 1974, 40 landless laborers applied individually for permission from the government to cultivate the khas land in Atgaon. The petitions were ignored.

Then in 1974, BRAC began its "functional education" classes in Atgaon. Those landless persons who participated became aware of their situation vis-à-vis the interests of others in the village. What emerged was the realization that to get the land from the government the landless would have to work together. Thus one night the landless of Atgaon, ranging in age from 25 to 70, came together and organized themselves into the Rajhasan Landless Cooperative Society. For the first time the landless were organized on the basis of common interest. Weekly cooperative meetings and village workshops, organized with the help of BRAC field workers, further heightened awareness of the social and economic realities of the village.

The cooperative then petitioned the government for the khas land. In 1976, after persistent pressure by the cooperative, the government finally granted the landless peasants 60 acres, amounting to one and one-half acres for each family. The village's well-off farmers became alarmed, for many of them were illegally using the khas land. They might have put up more resistance at this point if many had not been convinced that the poor lacked the wherewithal to cultivate the land profitably. The rich predicted that the land would eventually be mortgaged back to them anyway.

It's true that bringing the fallow land into cultivation requires a great deal of work and the purchase of seeds and good tools. But knowing its right to the land was secure, the cooperative was motivated to seek the credit it needed to get started. Lacking the proper collateral, it could not get credit from government agencies. But the cooperative was able to turn to BRAC, receiving a loan at 12 percent interest instead of the 50 to 200 percent interest demanded by the local moneylenders.

After much discussion, the cooperative decided to work the land as a collective farm, the first in the area. When the group had proved itself by actually leveling the land and planting the improved seed varieties, the large landlords started to worry. The success of the cooperative might instigate changes among other poor in the village. Moreover, if the cooperative succeeded there would be 40 fewer day laborers for the rich to hire. The well-to-do landlords, therefore, tried to thwart the cooperative by organizing other villagers to break the irrigation drainage canal on which the cooperative's land depended. They also tried to prevent the cooperative's use of river water for irrigation. But their efforts at sabotage failed. The rich landlords were divided. Those *not* occupying any of the khas land, and therefore not directly threatened by the cooperative's use of the land, were more sympathetic to the cooperative. They were mobilized against the efforts of the saboteur landlords.

Even though an early monsoon necessitated harvesting the crop before fully ready, the cooperative was able to pay back the entire BRAC loan plus interest. In 1977, the cooperative took out an even larger loan from BRAC and made arrangements with the government to purchase a power pump, normally possible only for the better-off farmers.

The members have also begun to work together in other economic activities—especially fishing during the rainy season. Furthermore, members of the cooperative participate in a health insurance program established by BRAC and are organizing for better childcare and health practices. In sharp contrast to pre-cooperative days, many of the landless families have decided to seek family planning assistance.

Over five years the changes in the lives of Atgaon's landless have followed this course: new literacy skills were gained in the process of achieving new awareness of the economic and social

The IDA is assisting with an irrigation and drainage project in Kekirawa district, Sri Lanka.

only through cooperative action could these limits be overcome. Cooperative action made possible the control of land which, for the first time, allowed some degree of self-determination and the ability to secure credit. This then opened doors to technical advances in production and the income necessary to participate in a health care system. The members of the co-operative are still poor. But real change has begun—and not only in their lives: the landless cooperative of Atgaon is now making contact with the landless in neighboring villages.

We in no way want to romanticize the work of any of the third world groups mentioned here. Helping to liberate the will and the capacity of people for self-determination is arduous and often risk-laden. Neither do we want to suggest that our list of U.S.-based groups that are on the right track is exhaustive. In addition to the Economic Development Bureau, Oxfam-America, the Unitarian-Universalist Service Committee and the American Friends Service Committee that we have mentioned, others, such as the Mennonite Central Committee and World Neighbors, have been commended for supporting indigenous development efforts, often against great odds. Again, we are not giving our approval or disapproval but are pointing to some of the groups that seem to be confronting many of the difficult questions we posed earlier. They are certainly worth examining.

Finally, we would ask you to compare the approach of the organizations we mention here—those trying not to go into another country with a pre-plan but to support local initiatives—with World Bank and AID projects described earlier. Mammoth official aid agencies can offer large sums of money but are structurally and ideologically incapable of helping the poor to confront the powerful forces blocking their development. Small, nongovernmental organizations do not require huge sums. The total annual budget of BRAC, covering work in literacy, health, and agricultural work in hundreds of villages, is about $300,000, compared, for example, to AID's $50 million electrification project in Bangladesh.

Highly selective voluntary aid, not official U.S. foreign aid, appears to be the channel through which direct American support for efforts of the poor in third world countries has a chance of helping, rather than hurting. Such aid should go to indigenous groups already based in village realities—using local field workers, starting with the most immediate problems at hand. It is a most difficult path but the only one through which outside aid can help the process of greater self-determination for those who now appear powerless to change their lives.

Just as we were completing this book, we learned of a moving incident witnessed by a friend and colleague. An official of a New York-based, international voluntary agency, who has devoted

Fruit vendor, Peshawar, Pakistan.

many years and tremendous effort to supporting progressive rural projects in Asia, participated in a study tour to a country that he had never before visited. The country had undergone a substantial redistribution of economic power and has a government committed to making health and education benefits available to everyone. He traveled far into the countryside and discovered, in one remote area, a modest but fully equipped clinic with responsible medical personnel serving the peasants.

Seeing this, he broke down and began to cry. Why was he so shaken? Because, he explained to his friends, he had worked for so many years supporting project after project and had never been able to achieve anything like what he was witnessing here. The difference, he understood, was that an entire economic and social structure had been changed. That was what made it possible. The experience caused him to rethink his own priorities.

Reflecting on this story, we are reminded that even the best voluntary aid efforts have the danger of absorbing all of our attention and of diluting our sense of responsibility for the role that both our government and corporations based in our economy play in maintaining unjust economic structures, structures that must be transformed before we can eliminate poverty and hunger.

20

What then is the appropriate response of those who want to help the hungry overseas?

RESPONSE Our most direct and critical response to needless hunger and suffering is our work to expose and to halt the multiple U.S. economic and military supports for repressive governments outlined in our response to Question 18. They block the struggle by the poor to control resources that are rightfully theirs.

There is a great danger, however, in thinking of our responsibility in terms of removing the obstacles in the way of people's efforts for greater justice. To speak of an "obstacle" is to conjure up a picture of something concrete and tangible. The forces that generate needless hunger can certainly be described, as we attempt to do in all of our work at the Institute for Food and Development Policy; one can identify economic and political power concentrating in fewer and fewer hands. But *why* are those forces allowed to continue? Here things are not so tangible.

We have come to see that part of what allows the forces causing needless suffering to continue is a web of assumptions so banal that most of us aren't even aware of them, much less challenging them. Built up over generations, these assumptions make the most outrageous injustices appear "normal" and, therefore, acceptable.

In the United States we accept as "normal," for example, that 6,000 "new" food items are introduced into the market each year and $20 million is spent on advertising to induce people to buy just one new snack food. This occurs while some poor and elderly people in our country find they have to survive on pet food! We accept as "normal" that a single corporation controls 100,000 acres of the country's prime farmland while a farm family, after having devoted generations to farming, must give up its farm because it doesn't have enough land to qualify for the size of loans a bank prefers to extend. We accept as "normal" that the United States, with its tremendous food-producing capacity, is importing more and more food from countries where the majority go hungry.

We must become sensitized to see the outrages in such normality. But we must also do more. We must ask *why*. We must examine the assumptions and habits woven into our day-to-day lives that, all added together, accept that normality. And then, we must ask how we can, piece by piece, target those assumptions.

Taking responsibility for the economic system

Too many of us have been led to believe that we must leave the economic system to the experts—and the experts (conveniently enough for them) turn out to be those people now in control. Others accept the notion that the economic system is magically controlled by rules of its own—"market" rules by which resources are allocated most "efficiently." But aren't both views merely different rationalizations for evading our responsibility for the economic system?

"magical" market forces nor by the decrees from those already controlling the society's wealth.

De-mystifying the experts

Thus a first step in answering "What can I do?" is to decide to stop accepting as *normal* surfeit for the few and deprivation for the many. So many of us, however, seem unable to do this. "Who are *we* to question the economic system?" "We're not economists." "It is so complicated." "Don't *they* know more?"

It is precisely such self-doubt that keeps the system going.

...work to expose and to halt the multiple U.S. economic and military supports for repressive governments...

The "economic" system is not something apart from our ordinary lives. It determines who eats and who starves; whether resources are utilized or whether they are neglected, whether they are conserved or destroyed.

In the economic system, as in any system, those who make the decisions do so in their own interests. The *only* way that the economic system will operate in the interests of the society as a whole is for the majority of people to participate in deciding how the society's resources are used and for whose gain. Economic decisions must therefore be made consciously, openly and democratically—not merely through

Thus, one of the most important lessons that we have had to learn is this: those who have been schooled and socialized to direct the powerful institutions that control our economic system are forced to accept and to work with*in* the system that creates hunger. Having become the beneficiaries of these institutions, they have been made unable to see outside of their boundaries. Their training, rather than preparing them to find solutions, has made them unable to ask the questions that could lead to solutions.

We say this not to condemn these individuals. The point is, rather, that we must not be intimidated. We must come to appreciate the fact that we need *not* be so trapped by the formulas and false assumptions drilled into those groomed to control our economic institutions. This may be the greatest asset we have.

But of course this does not mean that in our "primal innocence" we instinctively could do better. We are not advocating know-nothingism. Quite the contrary. If we want to both attack the forces that generate hunger and be able to build alternatives in our own lives, then we have to become sophisticated in areas that we previously thought were above our heads, esoteric, dull, unrelated to daily life. This means *educating* ourselves about those forces that generate and maintain hunger including those we discussed in our last response.

Lessons

The Institute for Food and Development Policy has produced a book entitled *What Can We Do?* The heart of the book is a series of interviews with people engaged in different kinds of food, land and hunger-related work all over North America. We asked them how and why they got involved. How do they see their work contributing to the profound changes necessary to end needless hunger? What keeps them going? We recommend the book to you. Our presumption is not that their answers will be your answers. Our intent is to give you a sense of the wide variety of options that are open to each of us in our own country, in our own communities.

In *What Can We Do?* we also draw out for our readers what we feel are some key lessons for those eager to take the leap from concern into action. Here we would like to summarize the points we have made in that book and in this concluding chapter:

1. Challenge "normality." Hunger exists in the face of plenty. We must not accept this outrageous "normality." Hunger is the product of the mundane workings of the economic system that so many accept as almost God-given. The first step is to stop taking it for granted!

2. Not a separate task. As long as we Americans acquiesce to the increasingly tight concentration of economic and, therefore, political power in our own society, can we expect the U.S. government, serving the interests of that economic elite, to put itself on the side of the less powerful abroad? Can we expect a society that allows a mere one percent of the food corporations to control 80 percent of the industry's assets to have a government that promotes redistribution of economic power elsewhere? Would a society in which only 45 corporations are permitted to control one-third of a leading agricultural state's best farmland be likely to have a government on the side of land redistribution abroad? Can a society which has the greatest food bounty in human history and yet millions of poor children measurably stunted from poor nutrition have a government that is an effective advocate abroad for everyone's right to food? We would be naive to think that it could or would. This means that all of our work to build a democracy in the United States is not a task separate from our work to end needless suffering abroad.

3. Take the initiative for change. Since those who hold power in our economic institutions and government were groomed to accept the boundaries of our economic system and have a vested interest in it, we must not look to them for the answers. Instead, we must trust the ability of "ordinary" people to see with fresher ideas; we have fewer vested interests; we are freer to start asking the big questions.

4. Take ourselves seriously. We can't effectively challenge the status quo unless we *know a great deal* about what we are trying to change. Therefore, we must apply ourselves with greater seriousness than ever before. In this process we must refuse to be intimidated by the mighty institutions whose officials want us to believe in their wisdom and our naivete.

5. Develop our analyses. Concern is not enough. Outrage is not enough. We have discovered that acting only out of these feelings can compound the very problems that we want to work to solve. We have, for example, seen how the natural human impulse "if they are hungry, send them our surplus food" has systematically under-cut the food security of people overseas. We must, therefore, always develop and apply our tools of analysis, as well as our hearts, as we try to attack the forces that generate hunger and to build an economic system based on human values. Throughout our lives, we must not just accumulate information but we must analyze, asking both "why?" and "why not?"

6. Seek not models but lessons. Looking for ideal models of human organization creates cynicism. There are *no* models; neither are there any ultimate solutions. While we believe that this is true we also know, from our own experience in other countries, that there are powerful lessons we can learn from the efforts of our counterparts in other countries. We must seek out those lessons, learn of and from their experiences. There *are* societies where people are asking fundamental questions such as: How can ordinary people take an active part in economic decision-making? How can planning take into account the need for participation and the need for coordination? Since there are no absolute answers to these kinds of questions, it is the development of a participatory, just *process* in which people can search and experiment that is the goal.

7. Focus. If we understood the common root of so many problems facing human beings today, we would not waste much time arguing with each other or with ourselves about which problem is most crucial to address. Address the problem that hits you (and the people you identify with) the hardest, the one that is most evident in your locale, the one *you* are the best equipped to address. Only you know what that is. It may not be a "food problem." It may relate to law, education, health, or energy. Each can be means through which one can attack the most basic question: How can we restructure our institutions so as to maximize rather than minimize the participation of those involved and make more equitable the distribution of rewards?

8. Believe in the possibility of change. It's hard to work toward a vision of something better without believing that change is possible. That seems obvious. But what allows us to believe that change is possible? Certainly part of the answer is discovering that much of the suffering we see today is not due to geographic or other physical givens but is the result of the actions of people. What people create, people can change.

We have also found that people who believe in the possibility of positive change in the world outside themselves have also experienced themselves changing. Thus "changing the world" must always involve *us* in a process of change. Personal change, of course means taking risks—committing ourselves beyond what we thought we were capable of doing.

Between Po and Ouagadougou, Upper Volta.

9. Work together. Change comes as a result of contact with others. Not only do we need others for the ongoing challenge that they represent, but for their help in our self-questioning in order to sharpen our unique contributions. We also must have the support of others when our risk-taking results in disappointments, as it inevitably will.

Thus, wherever we are, whoever we are, we must not be resigned to working alone. When we are working with others, we can experience daily the lessons of cooperative organization that reflect the transformation needed in the economic sphere.

10. Take the long view. Unless we can sense ourselves as part of an historical human struggle much longer than our lifetime, we are likely to be very disappointed and tempted to give up. The causes of needless hunger have been built and reinforced over hundreds and hundreds of years. Such forces, both the institutions and the assumptions on which they are based, cannot be changed in a few years or even in a few decades. Yes, dramatic new starts are achieved with apparent swiftness, such as the overthrow of a Somoza dictatorship or the defeat of Portuguese colonialism in Africa. But what appears as sudden is, in fact, the end result of years of hard work and sacrifice. Moreover, the rejection of the old does not create the new. That will take more years of work and sacrifice.

In researching and writing this book we have learned that U.S.-funded aid, focused on many of the world's most repressive governments, is not the appropriate response to the outrage of needless hunger. It claims to be attacking poverty. But poverty is an effect, not a cause. To get to the cause of poverty one must ask *why* people are poor. The answer is that they do not have the power to secure the income, food and housing that they need. To speak of power is to focus on relationships among people. Only by so focusing can we get to the roots of social problems. Official U.S. development assistance, however, cannot address the issue of power —the increasing concentration of control over food-producing resources—on a village and national level or on the level of international trade. It cannot because it must work with the very elites whose self-interest lies in maintaining the current structure of power right down to the village level. In addition, to raise the issue of the concentration of economic power in recipient countries would risk raising the issue at home. Powerful instruments of the U.S. government, tied so closely to U.S. corporate interests, cannot be expected to raise questions that might cause Americans to question the increasingly anti-democratic nature of our own economic system.

If power is the underlying issue and official development assistance is unable to confront it, how, then, can *we* confront it?

Part of the answer is that we cannot address the issue of power for other people. Just as we must confront the unjust concentration of economic and political power within our society, only the poor in the third world can organize to overcome their powerlessness. With this understanding and with the knowledge that in every country where many go hungry the poor are already struggling for a more just sharing of power, the appropriate role of Americans is to help remove the powerful obstacles in their way. As U.S. citizens we bear and must take responsibility for those obstacles— the economic, military and corporate supports for the structures of oppression—built with our tax and consumer dollars.

Learning that our government's aid is not on the side of the hungry, as we have documented throughout this book, might lead some to despair. For us, however, learning what is *not* the appropriate response to needless suffering—more U.S. government aid —has been a crucial first step in learning what *is* the appropriate response. We find hope and inspiration in the many groups around the country working to halt U.S. intervention on the side of oppressive forces in the third world and working to put themselves on the side of the poor. These groups range from those calling for a halt to U.S. aid for the Marcos regime in the Philippines to those raising money to support Nicaragua's development. (Appendix A lists some of these groups.)

The underlying theme of this book is power—particularly the lack of power of those who are needlessly hungry. While we hope this book has both shocked and outraged you, our central hope is that it has challenged you enough for you to want to discover the power that *you* have to make a contribution. The solution to these seemingly unsolvable world problems will only come as more of us make that discovery.

A PRIMER

Some Essential Facts about the Aid Establishment

World Bank headquarters, Washington, D.C.

Agency for International Development (USAID or AID)

AID is the principal agency administering U.S. bilateral aid.† The Agency was established by Congress in 1961. Until the bureaucratic reorganization of the foreign aid program in 1979, AID was part of the Department of State. Now it is the principal part of the International Development Cooperation Agency (IDCA),† an agency newly created to coordinate several U.S. government foreign aid programs including AID, the Institute for Scientific and Technical Cooperation, and the Overseas Private Investment Corporation.† The current administrator of AID is Douglas Bennett.

The programs administered by AID are the Economic Support Fund† (also called Security Supporting Assistance†), Functional Development Assistance, International Organizations and Programs, the Sahel Development Program, American Schools and Hospitals Abroad, International Disaster Assistance, Foreign Currency Programs, and Foreign Service Retirement Fund. AID also administers the U.S. food aid program,† although it is financed by the Department of Agriculture through the Commodity Credit Corporation.†

The total AID budget for fiscal year 1979 is approximately $3.718 billion. Since the passage of the New Directions† foreign aid legislation in 1973, AID's budget has more than *doubled*. The largest single component is the Economic Support Fund which comprises about half, or $1.9 billion, of the total budget.

The next largest component, Functional Development Assistance, accounts for about one third of the total AID budget, or $1.3 billion.

Under the Functional Development Assistance program, AID lends and grants funds for projects in foreign countries under the categories of Agriculture, Rural Development and Nutrition, Population Planning, Health, Education, Technical Assistance, Energy, Research, Reconstruction, and Selected Development Problems.

AID projects in a recipient country are designed by the AID "mission"—part of the "country team" of the U.S. embassy, approved by the Washington AID headquarters, and administered through the local government. Usually the recipient government is required to contribute "counterpart funds"† to cover local currency expenses of a project.

For several years preceding 1975, funds for projects under AID's Functional Development Assistance were approximately divided equally between grants and loans. More recently, grants have been increasing. In fiscal year 1979, almost 65 percent of the Functional Development Assistance was awarded as grants. Most of the funding provided through AID grants and loans comes with specific commercial conditions attached, usually restricting the recipients to purchase products and services from the United States. Almost three-quarters of the entire AID budget purchases products and services in the United States.

The leading recipient countries of AID program funds are listed in Chart II in our response to Question 2.

The administrative overhead of AID (Operating Expenses and the Foreign Service Retirement Fund, combined) totaled $282 million in fiscal year 1979, accounting for 7.5 percent of the total AID budget and equivalent to almost 18 percent of the Functional Development Assistance budget. Of the total Operating Expenses of $266.6 million, $100.2 million is for the Washington, D.C. headquarters and $166.4 million for overseas missions. AID directly employs 5,760 persons, at least 2,200 of whom are based in Washington. The conservatively estimated annual cost of one AID employee abroad is $84,000 in Africa and $62,500 in Latin America. In addition, AID (as well as the World Bank) employs thousands of consultants. No one knows how many.

Aid Program/Aid Project

Aid Program usually refers to a coordinated set of aid-financed activities or projects. For example, AID projects and administrative coordination apparatus in certain West African countries is called the Sahel Development Program. The section of the AID budget dealing with health care is also called a program. Other AID programs are Population Planning, Food and Nutrition, Education and Human Resources, and Selected Development Activities.

Aid Project is a single activity to generate specific results. A project may be sector or area specific, such as a road project or a regional development scheme. For major U.S.-funded programs, the project is the basic unit of management, usually with separate budget, plans and a limited time frame.

Program Lending. The World Bank in recent years has begun to make "non-project" loans (called Program Loans) to governments. These loans provide foreign exchange for both private and public sector imports deemed essential.

Basic Needs Strategy

By the late 1970s, "basic needs" had become the foremost buzzword in international development circles. In contrast with "traditional" or "trickle-down" approaches to development, "basic needs" strategy for economic development supposedly seeks to make the poor majority the *direct* targets of the development goals.

The roots of the new terminology can be traced to a 1976 World Employment Conference sponsored by the International Labor Organization. The ILO Director General's report, *Employment, Growth and Basic Needs: A One World Problem,* proposed to achieve "basic needs" satisfaction worldwide by the year 2000. Although not accepted by the Conference, in the months following the goal gained substantial endorsements from major policymakers. Robert McNamara of the World Bank addressed the Board of Governors in the fall of 1976, and presented the idea of a "global compact," having as its major objective "the meeting of the basic human needs of the ab-

solute poor in both the poor and middle income countries within a reasonable period of time, say by the end of the century." Academic and intellectual groups such as the Club of Rome and the Overseas Development Council then began to endorse "basic needs" approaches.

In early 1977, the administrator of AID, John Gilligan, endorsed "basic needs," saying that if the "international community" could gain the political will to "adopt an international strategy to meet minimum human needs—then we can eliminate absolute poverty in the world within the next generation." A subsequent endorsement came from the World Food and Nutrition Study of the National Academy of Sciences.

Implied in the statements of top policymakers is that "basic needs" can be met, without a fundamental restructuring of control over resources, through a shift in priorities and greater assistance from industrial countries. Always part of the new strategy is a call for greater quantities of aid.

Bilateral Aid

Bilateral aid refers to transfers of goods or services from one government to another, as either grants or loans. U.S. bilateral economic assistance programs include AID,† Food Aid† (P.L. 480), the Peace Corps, and the International Narcotics Control

Program. For details of U.S. bilateral military assistance, see our response to Question 18. Total U.S. bilateral economic and military aid was $7.6 billion in fiscal year 1979 ($5.3 billion in economic aid and $2.28 billion in military aid).

Not included in bilateral aid figures are other forms of direct economic support by the U.S. government for foreign governments and U.S. corporate operations overseas through the Export-Import Bank,† the Commodity Credit Corporation,† and the Overseas Private Investment Corporation.† These programs together far surpass the amount of official aid approved and reviewed by Congress. While total U.S. bilateral economic aid totaled $5.5 billion in 1978, the authorizations for loans, insurance and loan guarantee programs of the Export-Import Bank alone during the same year totaled $7.4 billion.

In 1978, the total amount of official development assistance from the Organization for Economic Cooperation and Development (OECD)† countries through bilateral channels was $13.1 billion. The total bilateral and multilateral aid from OECD countries was $18.8 billion. The total concessional assistance from the OPEC countries amounted to $3.7 billion in 1978, most of which was bilateral aid from Kuwait, Saudi Arabia and the United Arab Emirates. (See also Multilateral Aid.†)

Commodity Credit Corporation (CCC)

The CCC, a U.S. government corporation controlled by the Department of Agriculture, was established in 1956 to dispose of surplus agricultural commodities. It has become a primary means of developing foreign markets for U.S. agricultural exports. It also serves as a channel of support for friendly governments.

The CCC's Export Credit Sales Program issues medium and short-term credits at below international commercial lending rates to foreign purchasers of U.S.-produced agricultural commodities. Since 1956, the CCC has financed over $7 billion in such exports under this program. In 1978 alone, this program financed $1.6 billion in agricultural exports (or about six percent of total U.S. agricultural exports of $27.3 billion).

Offering interest-bearing credits for up to three years, the program is designed to supplement private export financing by extending credits to foreign purchasers where cash or privately financed sales are not possible. There is considerable debate, however, about whether CCC credits are, instead, displacing private financers. The Comptroller General's Office has reported that the gain in exports is "probably significantly less than the amount of credits granted," implying that many of the sales could have been financed privately.

In addition to its defined purpose of expanding export markets, the CCC also provides the Administration with a mechanism for significantly supporting foreign governments of its choosing. (See discussion of the CCC in Questions 12 and 18.)

Counterpart Funds

Bilateral or multilateral aid agencies do not usually *fully* fund projects in recipient countries. Instead, aid agencies grant or loan funds on the condition that matching funds—known as counterpart funds— are provided by the local government. The ratio of counterpart funds to those from an aid agency varies from project to project and with each agency. A foreign aid agency usually provides the foreign exchange component of the project. A typical World Bank irrigation scheme for Thailand is composed of an $80 million IBRD loan combined with $106 million worth of local currency provided by the government of Thailand. Overall, the World Bank (the IBRD and IDA) provided on average only 34 percent of the total cost of the projects it designed and financed during fiscal year 1979.

Many projects suffer from "implementation" delays when the local government has difficulty generating the counterpart funds for projects to which it is committed. In recent years some multilateral development banks have begun substantial local financing, that is, purchasing and

lending in local currencies in order to get around a local government's cash shortage.

Debt/Debt Service

Debt refers to public obligations of governments to each other, to lending agencies, and to private creditors. "Aid" substantially contributes to what has rapidly become an overwhelming debt burden for most underdeveloped countries, a burden approaching $200 billion, by 1979, for 75 non-oil-producing underdeveloped countries. Medium and long-term debt doubled between 1969 and 1973. Since then it has grown at an average annual rate of 21 percent. Not included in the $200 billion debt figure are short-term debts—known as current accounts deficits—which added $43 billion in 1979.

In 1975, the external public debt of the underdeveloped countries (including the oil-exporters) was divided thusly: 43 percent owed to individual governments, 16 percent to international (multilateral) organizations, and the remaining 41 percent to private suppliers of credit.

Debt service refers to payments on the principal and accrued interest on loans. Debt service for most underdeveloped countries has been mounting rapidly over the last decade. Many loans, granted as development aid, have come due. Also, the private transnational banks, offering shorter-term loans, have expanded their lending to underdeveloped countries. Such commercial lending has increased very rapidly, from less than half the total in 1970 to 60 percent in 1977.

Debt service has been rising much more rapidly than new aid receipts. As early as 1973, over 40 percent of the official aid from all the OECD countries was consumed by rising payments on matured loans. In 1977, the U.S. government, the world's largest public creditor, received almost as much in loan repayments from Latin America as it provided in new loans. The same pattern is evident with the multilateral lending agencies. Of the $3.4 billion lent to Latin America in 1977 by the Interamerican Development Bank and the World Bank, the banks received repayments on past loans equivalent to all but $450 million of the new loans. According to a top U.S. government official, "...of every new dollar made available in the year [1977] for Latin America through U.S. and international banks, Latin America's net take was seven cents."

Service on medium and long-term loans, which totaled $30 billion in 1976, is expected to increase tenfold to over $300 billion in 1990. By 1985, the debt servicing burden of the capitalist underdeveloped countries is expected to consume 88 percent of the loans received that year. That percentage is expected to rise to 90 percent by 1990.

Between 1974 and 1978, the number of countries which could not meet the debt payments due rose from three to 18. These 18 countries, all of which had experienced slower than anticipated growth in exports, had to seek multilateral debt renegotiation. In such a situation the International Monetary Fund (IMF), in concert with the World Bank, acts not only as a lender of last resort, but as an international financial auditor whose approval is essential to get further multilateral and private bank loans. Before getting such approval, a number of IMF-stipulated domestic economic measures must be carried out under IMF supervision. (See the IMF section in our response to Question 18 for details.)

Debt Service Ratio

The debt service ratio is a measure of the fiscal solvency of a country's economy. It com-

pares annual debt servicing payments with the annual total value of exports to reveal what portion of export earnings go for debt repayment. Private transnational banks usually restrict their lending to countries with a modest ratio: for countries producing raw materials, 10 to 15 percent; for more industrialized, "richer" countries, 15 to 20 percent. Many countries, however, are now exceeding these percentages. In 1977, for instance, Ghana had a ratio of 44 percent; Chile, 33 percent; Peru, 31 percent; and Bangladesh, 20 percent.

Development Assistance Committee (DAC)

See Organization for Economic Cooperation and Development

Economic Support Fund (ESF) (also called Security Supporting Assistance)

The ESF is the largest single component of the U.S. bilateral development assistance program, accounting over the last several years for just over one-half of all AID expenditures. Entirely composed of grants, ESF goes "to countries where U.S. interests can be served by bolstering economies which have been affected by political or economic crises," according to AID's Presentation to Congress (1980). "ESF is a flexible instrument which can finance balance of payments assistance,

cash transfers, commodity import programs, and large infrastructure projects—as well as development assistance programs of a more direct benefit to the poor." ESF funds are exempt from the "New Directions" guidelines passed by Congress.

Just two countries, Israel and Egypt, received 80 percent of the total $1.9 billion ESF budget for fiscal year 1979. Three other allied Middle East governments are recipients: Jordan, Syria and Turkey. The principal recipients outside the Middle East include Cyprus, Zambia, Botswana, the Philippines, Spain and Portugal.

Export-Import Bank (Eximbank)

The *Eximbank* is an independent U.S. federal agency authorized to make loans and issue loan guarantees and insurance to foreign governments and businesses for purchase of U.S. manufactured goods.

Sixty percent of Eximbank's

activities, in 1977, went for credit insurance for U.S. exporters, 21.9 percent for direct loans and financial guarantees, and 9.5 percent for guarantees to commercial banks that finance export activity.

More than 15 percent of all U.S. exports are supported through the Eximbank and related government programs. The proportion of exports subsidized by other industrial powers varies from 40 percent for Japan and Great Britain, to 30 percent for France, to only nine percent for West Germany and Canada.

The Eximbank was created by executive order, in 1934, to promote trade with the Soviet Union. Legislation today precludes the use of Eximbank funds for trade with either the Soviet Union or China.

(See the Eximbank section of our response to Question 18 for a more complete discussion.)

Food Aid

Food aid consists of agricultural commodities, invariably surpluses, from donor governments and agencies. Major food aid donors are the United States, Canada, the EEC (European Economic Community or "Common Market"), and the United Nations World Food Program as well as a number of private voluntary organizations (although they often obtain the food through a donor government's food aid program). Recipients may be either governments or individuals, depending on the program. Food aid may be granted or loaned, depending on the donor.

The U.S. food aid program (known as Food for Peace or P.L. 480, the Agricultural Trade Development Assistance Act) has three main categories, Titles I, II and III.

Title I, almost 60 percent of the total program, authorizes the sale of U.S. farm products to foreign governments on concessional terms (40 years at low interest). In fiscal year 1979, the program reached 31 countries and totaled $785 million (4.9 million tons of agricultural products). A government receiving Title I commodities may dispose of them in any way it chooses. Typically, the commodities are sold on commercial markets. The receipts from those sales are used for budgetary support for the government.

In proposed allocations for fiscal year 1980, the 10 top recipients of Title I funding are Egypt, India, Indonesia, Bangladesh, Pakistan, Portugal, South Korea, Peru, Haiti, and Sri Lanka. Together these 10 receive 54 percent of the total—$722 million out of $1,340.5 million.

Title II, approximately 40 percent of the total program, used $545 million worth of U.S. agricultural commodities in fiscal year 1979. Title II grants commodities and the means to transport them 1) to U.S. voluntary agencies such as CARE, Church World Service and Catholic Relief Services, 2) to the U.N.'s World Food Program, and 3) to a lesser extent, to recipient government programs for relief and other feeding programs in underdeveloped countries. In fiscal year 1979, U.S. agricultural commodities went to 81 countries through Title II programs.

The largest recipients of Title II P.L. 480 aid, in fiscal year 1978, were the governments of India, Egypt, Morocco, the Philippines and Bangladesh. Together they received 53 percent of all Title II aid—$167 million out of a total of $318 million.

Title III is called "Food for Development." One-year to five-year food aid supply agreements are signed between the United States and a recipient government which allow the proceeds from the sales of the commodities to be used for projects instead of being repaid by the recipient government. Title III agreements are now in effect with five countries: Bangladesh, Bolivia, Haiti, Honduras and Egypt.

Under P.L. 480, started in 1954, the United States has distributed more than $30 billion worth of surplus agricultural commodities. Over $20 billion has gone for cereal grains, $15 billion of that being for wheat and wheaten products.

The U.S. food aid program is jointly administered by the Department of Agriculture (USDA) and AID. P.L. 480 shipments are financed by USDA through the Commodity Credit Corporation (CCC).† (The CCC is a U.S. government corporation that issues medium and short-term credits for purchase of U.S. agricultural commodities.)

The United States has been the world's largest food aid donor but its share of total annual food aid has declined, from 96 percent in 1963 to 58 percent in 1975, partly as a result of the EEC's growing surpluses and the expansion of multilateral food aid under the U.N.'s World Food Program (WFP). On a global basis, food aid accounts for 12 to 16 percent of OECD official development assistance.

International Bank for Reconstruction and Development (IBRD)

See World Bank Group

International Development Association (IDA)

See World Bank Group

International Development Cooperation Agency (IDCA)

IDCA was formed during the 1979 restructuring of the U.S. foreign aid bureaucracy. It is an independent agency without a Cabinet-level post and is the agency which oversees AID, the

Overseas Private Investment Corporation (OPIC), and the newly created Institute for Scientific and Technical Cooperation. The director of IDCA is the principal foreign assistance advisor both to the President and to the Secretary of State. IDCA has an advisory role to the Treasury Department which retains authority for U.S. participation in the International Financial Institutions (IFIs).†IDCA is also responsible for U.S. participation in international development organizations such as the United Nations Development Program (UNDP).

International Finance Corporation (IFC)

See World Bank Group

International Financial Institutions (IFIs)

Also referred to as Multilateral Development Banks, the IFIs are international banks owned by member governments. They raise funds through members' contributions and by borrowing on international capital markets. They lend on concessional (easy) terms, principally to governments for economic development. The IFIs include the World Bank Group (the International Bank for Reconstruction and Development, the International Development Association, and the International Finance Corporation), the Asian Development Bank, the Inter-American Development Bank, and the African Development Fund. By 1979, the IFIs had committed $59 billion worth of loans, $34.5 billion of which has been dispersed. The World Bank Group accounts for 78 percent of total lending to date.

International Monetary Fund (IMF)

This 138-member international financial institution at the center of the world economy works to expand international trade, monetary convertibility and stability. As an international financial auditor and "lender of last resort," it wields considerable power over the domestic economic policies of member governments. The IMF, with a staff of 1,400, is headquartered in Washington, D.C. with offices in Paris and Geneva.

Membership in the IMF is a prerequisite for membership in the World Bank and the regional international financial institu-

tions. The IMF and the World Bank have a commn board of governors and hold annual meetings simultaneously.

(See our response to Question 18 for a more complete discussion of the impact of the IMF on countries' economic policies.)

Military Assistance

Details on military assistance and sales can be found in our response to Question 18.

Multilateral Aid

Multilateral aid is a transfer of goods or services from one government to another through an intermediary organization (controlled at least nominally by more than one government, hence "multilateral"). The principal intermediary agencies involved in multilateral aid are the World Bank† and the various regional international financial institutions† (Inter-American, African and Asian), the Witteveen Facility of the International Monetary Fund, and the various development organizations of the United Nations such as the United Nations Development Program (UNDP) and the World Food Program (WFP), as well as the International Fund for Agricultural Development (IFAD) set up by the 1974 World Food Conference.

Other multilateral aid institutions, namely the OPEC (Organization of Petroleum-Exporting Countries) Special Fund, the Arab Fund for Economic and Social Development, and the Islamic Development Bank, have been established by the oil exporting countries. OPEC constitutes a significant source of concessional finance, with disbursements of $2.8 billion in 1978, compared to $18.8 billion from the OECD† countries. (The level of OPEC aid has dropped from $5.37 billion in 1976, in large part reflecting the major cutback in OPEC aid flows to Egypt.)

Of the total $18.8 billion in official development assistance in 1978, $13.1 billion was in bilateral aid and $5.7 billion in multilateral aid.

Multilateral aid, which consists almost entirely of loans, usually on varied concessional terms, contrasts with bilateral aid which is generally a mix of grants and loans.

For fiscal year 1979, the Carter administration proposed a $3.6

billion U.S. appropriation for the World Bank Group, the Asian Development Bank, the Inter-American Development Bank, and the African Development Fund. The largest recipient of U.S. commitments and contributions was the World Bank Group ($2.1 billion).

The term multilateral aid is not used to refer to government aid through private voluntary organizations.

New Directions

In 1973, legislation was passed requiring AID to focus more of its efforts on helping the poor majority in underdeveloped countries. Post-1973 AID programs that claim to fulfill this mandate are called *New Directions*.

In 1975, the New Directions legislation was extended and consolidated into the International Development and Food Assistance Act. This legislation reinforced the mandates for "appropriate technology," "participation of the poor," "basic human needs," and "bottom-up" rather than "top-down" approaches to development. The 1973 and 1975 aid reforms were intended to steer U.S. bilateral development aid away from the discredited "trickle-down" approach and toward programs that directly address the problems of rural poverty. Subsections 102(c) and (d) require standards for measuring progress according to the New Directions goals. These subsections specify that "greatest emphasis" in U.S. aid programs is to be given to "countries and activities which effectively involve the poor in development" and which "help the poor toward a better life." Also added in the 1975 legislation were provisions to deny U.S. bilateral aid to countries "with consistent patterns of gross violations of internationally recognized human rights."

The Economic Support Fund —accounting for about half of the total AID funds—is exempt from the New Directions guidelines. Neither do New Directions guidelines apply to the separately funded contributions from the United States to multilateral development banks, which comprise the largest form of U.S. development aid.

Organization for Economic Cooperation and Development (OECD)

This economic policy coordination "club," originally composed of the nonsocialist European countries, was formed following World War II. In 1961, it was expanded to include Canada, the United States, Australia, New Zealand, and Japan. At the same time a special committee, the Development Assistance Committee (DAC),† was created to promote and coordinate bilateral aid programs. Many global statistics on aid programs group the "DAC countries" together.

The OECD members are: Australia, Austria, Belgium, Canada, Denmark, Finland, France, Germany, Greece, Iceland, Ireland, Italy, Japan, Luxembourg, the Netherlands, New Zealand, Norway, Portugal, Spain, Sweden, Switzerland, Turkey, the United Kingdom and the United States.

Overseas Private Investment Corporation (OPIC)

OPIC is an insurance program backed by the U.S. government for investments by U.S. corporations abroad. It also loans directly to corporations for investment in third world countries and shares in the costs of "preinvestment" surveys. In 1978, 40 percent of OPIC's assistance went to the manufacturing sector, 20 percent to agribusiness, and 14 percent to banking.

In 1979, OPIC along with AID was made part of a new umbrella agency, the International Development Cooperation Agency (IDCA).†

See our response to Question 18 for a more complete discussion of the role of OPIC.

Private Voluntary Organizations (PVOs or Volags)

PVOs are private, not-for-profit, tax-exempt nongovernmental organizations established and governed by private citizens whose purpose is to engage in voluntary, charitable relief and development assistance overseas. Among the PVOs are foundations, religious organizations, and other not-for-profit groups. Aid from PVOs is given in the form of commodities, project support, and services to support both government and nongovernment programs. U.S. PVOs work in almost every country in the world, including some countries where there is no U.S. bilateral aid† program.

Over the past 15 years there has been a rapid expansion of dollar amounts of aid channeled through U.S. PVOs. Levels of PVO aid increased from $422 million in 1964 to $1,084 million in 1979.* Three-fifths of this increase is attributable to private sector contributions. The balance is supplied by U.S. government contributions. Of the $477 million U.S. government contribution in 1978, two-thirds was in the form of P.L. 480 food commodities and related ocean freight costs, funded by the Department of Agriculture and administered by AID.† AID also provides grants and contracts to PVOs for development projects, population programs and research —$720 million worth between 1968 and 1978. AID grants to PVOs were expanded under the New Directions† foreign aid

---

* These figures do not include the aid going through some 2,000 to 3,000 private international assistance programs not registered with the U.S. State Department. Their yearly dispursements overseas exceed $400 million.

legislation which established an Office of Private and Voluntary Cooperation within AID to award grants to PVO overseas programs. Since 1974, $125 million in grant support has been channeled to PVO overseas programs.

Many PVOs have become heavily dependent on U.S. government contributions. Catholic Relief Services (CRS) had a 1978 budget of $257 million; about $179 million came from the U.S. government ($126 million in food, $46 million to ship food overseas, and $7 million in grants for development projects). In 1979, CRS obtained $500,000 for its New York headquarters' overhead. Eighty percent ($165 million) of CARE's $207 million budget came from similar U.S. government sources.

On a worldwide level, PVO aid reached $1,489 million in 1977, with the largest donations from the United States, West Germany, Canada, United Kingdom, Sweden and the Netherlands. In 1977, nongovernment aid programs represented 9.2 percent of the total public and private aid from all OECD countries.

Tied Aid

Over one-half of grants and credits from the nonsocialist nations are *tied* to the condition that they be used for purchases from the donor country. This restriction applies solely to bilateral aid. The degree to which aid donors tie their aid varies: in 1977, Italy tied only 19 percent of its bilateral aid. The United States, at the other end of the spectrum, tied 72 percent of all its bilateral assistance.

In the United States, the tying of aid has been viewed as a way to boost exports to support the balance of payments and as a way to gain the support of big business lobbyists for the foreign aid program.

Tying aid means that the recipient government cannot shop around for the most appropriate product and the best price.

World Bank Group

The World Bank Group is the largest of the multilateral development banks and lending institutions for development financing. Combined annual lending exceeded $10 billion in 1979. In addition, co-financing of Bank-designed projects by other lending agencies (bilateral and multilateral) and by private, commercial banks adds to the significance of the World Bank's lending. In 1978, co-financing of 79 projects augmented the Bank's lending by $2.4 billion.

The Group is composed of three operating entities: the International Bank for Reconstruction and Development (IBRD or World Bank), the International Development Association (IDA), and the International Finance Corporation (IFC). Each entity is a country-membership organization and lends money for development projects to member countries. Each entity's source of funds differs, however, as does the interest rate each charges.

The IBRD is the largest of the World Bank Group entities, making long-term loans to underdeveloped countries generally at somewhat less than the commercial bank rate. Loans are made only to foreign governments and, with rare exceptions, are designated for the foreign exchange component of the economic development projects designed by the IBRD staff and the borrowing government.

The IBRD was originally chartered at the close of World War II as a mechanism for financing the reconstruction of war-devastated Europe. During the 1950s the focus of IBRD lending shifted to third world development projects.

In 1979, 27 percent of total IBRD lending went to countries where per capita incomes were $580 or less.

IBRD loans have gone predominantly to develop roads, dams, power plants, telecommunications, ports and railways—thereby facilitating the growth of private (often foreign) corporations in industry and mining. The 1970s saw a growth in lending for "Agriculture and Rural Development," representing 22 percent of IBRD loans in fiscal year 1979. (See our response to Question 5 for an examination of the Bank's "Agriculture and Rural Development" lending.) Other lending areas emphasized in recent years include population planning, education, tourism, technical assistance, and water supply.

In 1979, IBRD lending totaled $7 billion to 142 projects in 44 countries.

The IBRD is owned by the now 134 member countries which subscribe to the capital stock of the Bank. Member country "subscriptions" are in part paid and in part pledged. Thus the IBRD receives both money and promises of money from member governments. The IBRD then uses this paid-in and "callable" capital as the basis upon which to borrow money on commercial bond markets.

Interest-bearing IBRD bonds are sold through commercial bond markets to investment companies, to institutional investors of all kinds including churches and universities, to banks and insurance companies, and to governments and private citizens.

Control. In theory the IBRD is run by a board of governors, with each of the 134 member countries represented on the board. Control effectively rests, however, with the 20 executive directors. Management of the day-to-day operations of the IBRD is controlled by the president, who chairs meetings of the executive directors and is *selected by the President of the United States*, the largest shareholder in the Bank. Since 1978, Robert McNamara, formerly U.S. Secretary of Defense and before that the president of the Ford Motor Company, has been president of the IBRD.

Voting power in the IBRD depends on each country's capital subscription. Thus the United States has the greatest voting power, 21.48 percent of the total. The United States has pledged approximately $9 billion to IBRD, including $894 million in paid capital. Several major U.S. allies also have sizable voting power: United Kingdom, 8.12 percent; West Germany, 5.52 percent; Japan, 4.26 percent; and France, 4.0 percent. This concentration of voting power means that the United States and its principal allies easily hold an effective veto; in practice the Bank does not bring to a vote any item on which there is not prior consensus.

Membership. Neither the Soviet Union nor allied Eastern European countries are members of the IBRD or of the International Monetary Fund (IMF) (which is a prerequisite to membership in the IBRD). Yugoslavia has long-standing membership. The People's Republic of China is scheduled soon to become a member of the IMF and the IBRD.

Profits. Despite the fact that it lends at less than market rates of interest, the IBRD has continuously been a profit-making operation. In fiscal year 1979, the IBRD had a net income of $407 million on gross revenues of $2.4 billion. The IBRD divides its profits between its reserve funds and its grants to the IDA. In fiscal year 1978, of the $238 million in profits earned by the IBRD, $138 million were allocated to the Gen-

eral Reserve (totalling $2.2 billion) and $100 million to the IDA.

The World Bank has organized consortia or consultative groups of aid donors for the following countries: Colombia, Ethiopia, Ghana, Bangladesh, India, Korea, Malaysia, Morocco, Nigeria, Pakistan, Peru, the Philippines, Sri Lanka, Sudan, Thailand, Tunisia, Zaire, Kenya, Uganda and Tanzania. The Bank also serves as chief advisor to the Intergovernmental Group on Indonesia, chaired by the Netherlands.

IDA is the next largest World Bank Group entity. IDA was established in 1960, to provide development finance in much the same manner as the IBRD but specifically for "low income" countries. IDA's aid is called credits rather than loans because of the minimal service charge and the long grace period. For this reason IDA is commonly referred to as the "soft loan window" of the World Bank. IDA credits are

limited to countries with a per capita GNP of less than $581 (1977 dollars). About 50 countries qualify for IDA credits under the current per capita GNP criterion.

IDA is open to all members of the IBRD and, in 1979, there were 121 member countries. Like the IBRD, IDA extends credits for development projects, usually covering the foreign currency portions of the project. IDA made new commitments during 1979, exceeding $3 billion, to 43 countries for 105 projects.

The method of funding IDA is different from that of the IBRD. Member countries are divided into "Part I" and "Part II" countries. Part I countries contribute to IDA through government appropriations. Part II countries receive IDA credits and, therefore, all have per capita GNPs of less than $581. IDA also receives some of the operating profit of the IBRD.

Voting power in IDA is based on a country's subscriptions and provision of supplementary resources. In 1978, Part I countries had 96 percent of the voting power.

The United States has been the largest supplier of funds to IDA, providing over $5.6 billion in capital stock subscriptions and "supplementary resources" that are also known as "replenishment." The largest recipients of IDA credits over its history have been India (with 41 percent of the total), Bangladesh (7 percent), Pakistan (6.3 percent), Indonesia (4.5 percent), Tanzania (2.5 percent), and the Sudan (2 percent).

IDA credits go to the same economic sectors as IBRD loans. These sectors include agriculture and rural development, power, and. transportation, to name a few. In fiscal year 1979, 32 percent of IDA lending went for agriculture and rural development.

Although legally and financially distinct from the IBRD, IDA is administered by the same staff.

N.B. Neither the IBRD nor IDA supplies all the funds for the development projects they design with recipient governments. In 1979, IBRD and IDA lending for projects provided an average of 34 percent for project costs. The balance (counterpart funds†) was provided by the recipient.

The IFC is the third operating entity of the World Bank Group. It was established in 1956, "to assist the economic development of less developed countries by promoting growth in the private sector of their economies and helping to mobilize domestic and foreign capital for this purpose" (Annual Report). The IFC has 109 members. Membership in the IBRD is a prerequisite for membership in the IFC. Like IDA and the IBRD, the IFC supports projects. Support, however, is not limited to loans. The IFC can buy shares in a private corporate venture or extend credit to a private corporation without any government guarantees. In addition, the IFC can promote investment projects by "identifying and bringing together investment opportunities and qualified investors" (Annual Report). It also supports the development of local capital markets and financial institutions in developing countries and offers technical assistance to governments to encourage "productive and beneficial domestic and foreign investment."

In fiscal year 1979, the IFC made 48 investments totaling $425 million. About half of those investments were in countries with per capita incomes less than $520 per year. Over half of the IFC investments were for manufacturing. The second largest amount went for "agribusiness."

The IFC raises most of its funds through "capital subscriptions" of the industrial member countries, upon which voting power is based. The United States has 37.6 percent of the voting power; the United Kingdom, 10 percent; West Germany, 6.6 percent. It also sells "participations" in its loans mostly to commercial banks. In 1978, the IFC's gross income was $71 million; its net income was $12.5 million.

NOTES

Question 1

1. *AID Congressional Presentation, Fiscal Year 1980,* p. 29. AID also uses the term "functional development assistance" to refer to that part of its budget going to agriculture, rural development, nutrition, population, health education and human resources projects as well as projects in the Sahel.
2. Ibid., pp. 27-31.
3. *AID Congressional Presentation, Fiscal Year 1979,* main volume, pp. 139G-139I.
4. *AID Congressional Presentation, Fiscal Year 1980,* main volume, pp. 29-30.
5. *Foreign Assistance and Related Agencies Appropriations for 1980,* Part 2, hearings before a House subcomm. of the Comm. on Approp., 96th Cong., 2nd Sess., pp. 706-707.
6. *AID Congressional Presentation, Fiscal Year 1980,* main volume, p. 12.
7. Ibid., p. 5. See also AID, *Annual Foreign Assistance Report,* Part 2, Foreign Assistance Provided by the U.S. Government to Foreign Countries and International Organizations by Category and Country (Washington: AID, revised March 1979), Table I-A.
8. The World Bank, for example, defined a low-income country in 1978 as one with $250 per capita GNP or less. See World Bank, *World Development Report* (Washington: World Bank, 1978).
9. AID, *Annual Foreign Assistance Report,* Part 2, Table I-A.

Question 2

1. Department of State, *Report on Human Rights Practices in Countries Receiving U.S. Aid,* submitted to the Senate Comm. on Foreign Relations and the House Comm. on Foreign Affairs, February 8, 1979. See also Center for International Policy, *Human Rights and the U.S. Foreign Assistance Program, Fiscal Year 1978,* Part 2—East Asia (Washington: Center for International Policy, 1977).
2. International Labor Office, *Poverty and Landlessness in Rural Asia* (Geneva: International Labor Office, 1977), pp. 206-208, 218-219.
3. World Bank, *Indonesia: Appraisal of a Nutrition Development Project,* Report No. 1318-IND (Washington: World Bank, Feb. 16, 1977), Annex 1, p. 1.
4. *Poverty and Landlessness in Rural Asia,* pp. 210-212.
5. "Indonesia: A short-term oil boom, long-term problems," *Business Week,* Dec. 17, 1979, p. 42.
6. AID, *Annual Budget Submission FY 1979, USAID Indonesia,* Annex (Washington: AID, June 1977), p. 24. See also Center for International Policy, *Indonesia: Economic Prospects and the Status of Human Rights* (Washington: Center for International Policy, 1976), and *Human Rights. . .East Asia.*
7. *Human Rights. . .East Asia,* p. 13.
8. *Amnesty International Report 1979* (London: Amnesty International Publications), p. 105.
9. Ibid.
10. Nick Mottern, "Indicators of Political Instability in Pakistan and Advisability of Providing U.S. Assistance," unpublished document based on interviews carried out in February, 1980.
11. S.M. Naseem, "Rural Poverty and Landlessness in Pakistan," in *Poverty and Landlessness in Rural Asia,* esp. pp. 52-57.
12. Ibid., esp. pp. 42-47.

13. Ibid., p. 48.

14. Ibid., pp. 43-46. See also *Pakistan: Operational Implications of Adopting Basic Needs Targets* (Washington: World Bank, Dec. 2, 1977).

15. *Pakistan: Operational Implications.*

16. Ibid.

17. Ibid.

18. Institute of Nutrition and Food Science, *Nutritional Survey of Rural Bangladesh 1975-1976* (Dacca, Bangladesh: U. of Dacca, Dec. 1977).

19. World Bank, *Bangladesh: Current Trends and Development Issues* (Washington: World Bank, Dec. 15, 1978), pp. 24, 29-30, 87.

20. Qazi Kholiquzzaman Ahmad, "Rural Development in Bangladesh—Some Reflections on the Current Scenario," speech presented at the Second Annual Conference of Bangladesh Krishi Arthanitibeed Samity, Dacca, January 12-13, 1980, p. 4. Available from the Bangladesh Institute for Development Studies, Dacca. (The precise contrast is between 1972/73 and 1977/78 in constant 1972/73 dollars.) See also Michael Scott, *Aid to Bangladesh: For Better or Worse?* an interview (San Francisco: Inst. for Food and Develop. Policy, 1979), and Betsy Hartmann and James Boyce, *Needless Hunger: Voices from a Bangladesh Village* (San Francisco: Inst. for Food and Develop. Policy, 1979).

21. *Human Rights...East Asia,* p. 38.

22. Ho Kwon Ping, "The Mortgaged New Society," *Far Eastern Economic Review,* June 29, 1979, pp. 51-55.

23. Ho Kwon Ping, citing the Asian Development Bank.

24. *Human Rights...East Asia,* pp. 27-30.

25. Ho Kwon Ping, "A long time laying the cornerstone," *Far Eastern Economic Review,* June 29, 1979, p. 56.

26. Filipino Information Service (FILINS) (P.O. Box 12215, San Francisco, CA 94112), No. 3, p. 5.

27. David Wurfel, "Philippine Agrarian Policy Today: Implementation and Political Impact," mimeo (Windsor, Ontario: U. of Windsor, 1977).

28. *Philippine Liberation Courier,* Vol. 4, No. 1 (Jan. 1980), p. 10.

29. George McT. Kahin, "The Need to End Our Risky Military Ties to Manila," *Washington Post,* Aug. 27, 1978. See also *Foreign Assistance and Related Programs Appropriations for 1980,* hearings before a House subcomm. of the Comm. on Approp., 96th Cong., 1st Sess., April 6, 1979, "Philippine Base Rights," pp. 275-322. Originally President Carter promised President Marcos $500 million in military assistance over a five-year period. In April 1978, Rep. Lester L. Wolff persuaded the Administration to shift $200 million of this to economic assistance, according to Jim Morrell of the Center for International Policy in "Attacking Philippines Poverty with Guns," *Newsday,* March 11, 1980.

30. "Preparing for Revolution: The United Front in the Philippines," *Southeast Asia Chronicle,* No. 62 (May-June 1978).

31. Milton Esman and Associates, *Landlessness and Nearlandlessness in Developing Countries* (Ithaca, N.Y.: Rural Development Committee, Center for International Studies, Cornell U.), p. 210.

32. Planning Commission, *Draft Five-Year Plan 1978-1983* (New Delhi: Government of India), p. 3.

33. Esman, *Landlessness and Nearlandlessness in Developing Countries,* p. 213.

34. Michael Klare, *Supplying Repression: U.S. Support for Authoritarian Regimes Abroad* (Washington: Inst. for Policy Studies, 1977), p. 40. See also *Arming the Third World* (Philadelphia: NARMIC, February 1979), and *AID Congressional Presentation, Fiscal Year 1979,* main volume, p. 139-I.

35. *Amnesty International Report 1978* (London: Amnesty International Publications). See also *International Human Rights and the Administration's Security Assistance Program for Fiscal Year 1979: A Critique* (Washington: Coalition for a New Foreign and Military Policy, 1978).

Question 3

1. Barry Newman, "The Greening of

Java Produces More Rice, But Problems Persist," *Wall Street Journal,* June 14, 1978.

2. Gunnar Myrdal, *Need for Reforms in Underdeveloped Countries,* S-106 91 (Stockholm: Inst. for International Economic Studies, 1978), p. 35.

3. AID, *Overseas Loans and Grants and Assistance from International Organizations, Obligations and Loan Authorities, July 1, 1945—September 30, 1978* (Washington: AID), p. 56.

4. Alan Riding, "Behind U.S. Aid to Salvador," *San Francisco Chronicle,* February, 1980, p. 10.

5. *AID Congressional Presentation, Fiscal Year 1979,* main volume, p. 139-H.

6. Center for International Policy, *Human Rights and the U.S. Foreign Assistance Program, Fiscal Year 1978, East Asia* (Washington: Center for International Policy, 1977), pp. 63, 68.

7. Michael Klare, *Supplying Repression: U.S. Support for Authoritarian Regimes Abroad* (Washington: Inst. for Policy Studies, 1977), pp. 10, 26.

8. *Human Rights...East Asia,* pp. 67-69 and *AID Congressional Presentation, Fiscal Year 1979,* p. 139-A.

9. Joseph Collins, *Agrarian Reform and Counter-Reform in Chile* (San Francisco: Inst. for Food and Develop. Policy, 1979).

Question 4

1. World Bank, *World Development Report 1978* (Washington: World Bank), p. 76.

2. Bill Freund, "Oil Boom and Crisis in Contemporary Nigeria," *Review of African Political Economy,* No. 13 (Aug.-Nov. 1978), pp. 91ff.

3. *World Bank Annual Report 1979,* pp. 95-96.

4. Center for International Policy, *World Bank Sets $2.9 Billion in Loans to Human Rights Violators for Fiscal Year 1979* (Washingon: Center for International Policy), p. 2.

5. *World Bank Annual Report 1979,* p. 27.

6. For an excellent examination of the political economy of Zaire, see Guy Gran, ed., *Zaire: The Political Economy of Underdevelopment* (New York: Praeger, 1979).

7. *World Bank Annual Report 1979,* p. 185.

8. World Bank, *Report and Recommendation of the President of the International Development Association to the Executive Directors on a Proposed Credit to the Republic of Zaire for an Ituri Livestock Development Project,* Report No. P-1964-ZR (Washington: World Bank, March 30, 1977).

9. Food and Agriculture Organization, *The Fourth World Food Survey,* FAO Statistics Series No. 11, FAO Food and Nutrition Series No. 10 (Rome: Food and Agriculture Organization, United Nations, 1977), p. 128.

10. Irving Kaplan, ed., *Zaire: A Country Study* (Washington: Foreign Areas Studies, American University, May, 1978), p. xxiii.

11. "Zaire: an IMF Subsidiary?" *The International Bulletin,* Vol. 6, No. 3 (Feb. 12, 1979), p. 2.

12. *Manchester Guardian Weekly,* June 11, 1978.

13. World Bank, *Zaire: Appraisal of the Oil Palm Project,* Report No. 1592-ZR (Washington: World Bank, 1978), p. i.

14. *Foreign Assistance and Related Programs Appropriations for 1980,* hearings before a House subcomm. of the Comm. on Approp., 96th Cong., 1st Sess., Part 2, International Financial Institutions, p. 10.

15. Steven Arnold and Linda Smith, "The Impact of the InterAmerican Development Bank upon the Poor in Latin America," paper prepared for the National Convention of the Latin American Studies Association, Pittsburgh, April 5-7, 1979.

16. *Foreign Assistance...for 1980,* pp. 173-174.

17. Ibid., pp. 180-183.

18. Ibid., pp. 182-183.

Question 5

1. Cyrus Vance, former Secretary of State, "Foreign Assistance and U.S. Foreign Policy," speech to the National Convention of the League of Women Voters, May 1, 1978; and

"America's Commitment to Third World Development," speech to the Northwest Regional Conference on the Emerging World Order, March 30, 1979. Both are available from Bureau of Public Affairs, Dept. of State. See also Cyrus Vance, "U.S. Aid Programs, FY 80," statement before the House Foreign Affairs Comm., Feb. 5, 1979.

2. *AID Congressional Presentation, Fiscal Year 1979,* main volume, p. 8.

3. Judith Tendler, *Rural Electrification: Linkages and Justifications,* AID Programs Evaluation Discussion Paper No. 3 (Washington: Studies Division, Office of Evaluation, AID, 1979), p. 5.

4. Ibid., p. 15.

5. Ibid., p. 18.

6. Ibid., p. 21.

7. Ibid., p. xi.

8. *AID Congressional Presentation, Fiscal Year 1979,* Annex A, p. 481.

9. AID agricultural program officer, interview by staff of Inst. for Food and Develop. Policy, Jakarta, Indonesia, Feb., 1978.

10. Barry Newman, "Do Multinationals Really Create Jobs in the Third World?" *Wall Street Journal,* Sept. 25, 1979.

11. AID, *Indonesia—Rural Electrification I,* No. 497-0267, Volume II (Washington: AID, Aug. 1977), Annex G-1, p. 3.

12. Walden Bello, Peter Hayes, and Lyuba Zarsky, "500 Mile Island: The Philippine Nuclear Reactor Deal," *Pacific Research,* Vol. 10, No. 1 (1979).

13. Roy Prosterman, "Executive Report to the Steering Comm. on Post Harvest Operations of the Government of Bangladesh Task Force on Rice Processing and By-Products Utilization," (Feb. 16, 1978). Cited in *Foreign Assistance and Related Programs Appropriations for 1980,* hearings before a House subcomm. of the Comm. on Approp., 96th Cong., 1st Sess., Part 1, p. 924.

14. Center for Latin American Studies, *Rural Electrification: An Evaluation of Effects on Economic and Social Changes in Costa Rica and Colombia* (Gainesville: University of Florida, Aug. 31, 1973).

15. AID, *Bangladesh—Rural Electrification,* Project Paper: Proposal and Recommendations for the Review of the Development Loan Committee, AID-DLC/P-2232 (Washington: AID, 1977).

16. AID Mission, interview by staff of the Inst. for Food and Develop. Policy, Dacca, Bangladesh, Jan. 1978.

17. *AID Congressional Presentation, Fiscal Year 1979,* Annex A, p. 508.

18. Ibid., p. 733.

19. Ibid., p. 330.

20. Roy Prosterman and C.A. Taylor, "Grading Bureaucratic Compliance: A Briefing Paper on AID's Fiscal Year 1977 Presentation to Congress," unpublished manuscript, March 11, 1976, pp. 12ff.

21. *Foreign Assistance. . .for 1980,* Part I, testimony of Roy Prosterman, p. 923.

22. Michael Scott, *Aid to Bangladesh: For Better or Worse?* (San Francisco: Oxfam-America and the Inst. for Food and Develop. Policy, 1979.)

23. *AID Congressional Presentation, Fiscal Year 1979,* Annex A, p. 251.

24. Ibid., p. 529.

25. Frances Moore Lappé and Joseph Collins, *Food First: Beyond the Myth of Scarcity* (New York: Ballantine, 1979), see Part 10, Food Self Reliance, pp. 455-504.

26. Mahbub ul Haq, "Changing emphasis of the Bank's lending policies," *Finance & Development,* Vol. 15, No. 2 (June 1978), p. 12ff. See also testimony of Hon. W. Michael Blumenthal, Sec. of the Treasury, before the House subcomm. on foreign operations and related operations and related programs of the Comm. on Approp. in *Foreign Assistance. . .for 1980,* Part 6, International Financial Institutions, pp. 1-84.

27. *Foreign Assistance. . .for 1980,* Part 6, International Financial Institutions, p. 47.

28. AID agricultural program officer, interview by staff of Inst. for Food and Develop. Policy, Jakarta, Indonesia, Feb. 1978.

29. World Bank, *Appraisal of the Maradi Rural Development Project: Niger,*

Report No. 881a-NIR (Washington: World Bank, Nov. 14, 1975), p. 21.

30. World Bank, *Staff Appraisal Report: Northeast Brazil, Bahia Rural Development Project—Paraguacu,* Report No. 2009a-BR (Washington: World Bank, May 19, 1978), p. 35.

31. World Bank, *Appraisal Report: Northeast Brazil, Paraiba Rural Development Project—Brejo,* Report No. 1914-BR (Washington: World Bank, March 10, 1978), p. 18.

32. World Bank, *Thailand: Appraisal of the National Agricultural Extension Project,* Report No. 1256a-TH (Washington: World Bank, March 10, 1977), pp. 14, 15, Annex 10, Table 3.

33. World Bank, *Appraisal of Integrated Rural Development Project—Pider, Mexico,* Report No. 6601-ME (Washington: World Bank, April 16, 1975), p. 9.

34. World Bank, "Rural Development Project, Credit 631-BD, Project Review Report and Action Program," Office Memorandum (Washington: World Bank, Sept. 19, 1977), pp. 7-8.

35. Barry Newman, "Missing the Mark: In Indonesia, Attempts by World Bank to Aid Poor Often Go Astray," *Wall Street Journal,* Nov. 10, 1977, p. 1.

36. Walden Bello and Severina Rivera, ed., *The Logistics of Repression and Other Essays* (Washington: Friends of the Filipino People), pp. 107-110.

37. Richard Rhoda, *Development Activities and Rural-Urban Migration: Is it Possible to Keep Them Down on the Farm?* (Washington: Office of Urban Development, Bureau for Development Support, AID, March 1979), p. 53.

Question 6

1. *World Bank Annual Reports 1973-1979.*

2. *New York Times,* April 2, 1978, p. E-3.

3. "Brazil neglects rural labor and land —World Bank," *Latin American Economic Report,* Vol. V, No. 42 (Oct. 28, 1977), p. 192.

4. Dom Jose Rodrigues De Souza, interview by representatives of Misereor, Sept. 1, 1978.

5. "Brazil neglects rural labor...," p. 192.

6. Sheilah Ocampo, "The Battle for Chico River," *Far Eastern Economic Review,* Oct. 20, 1978, p. 32.

7. World Bank, *Report on Tarabela Dam Project (Pakistan),* July-Aug. 1975, cited in Susan George, *How the Other Half Dies* (Montclair, N.J.: Allenheld, Osmun and Co., 1977).

8. Cheryl Payer, *The Debt Trap: The IMF and the Third World* (New York: Monthly Review Press, 1974); see esp. Appendix 1.

9. World Bank document cited by Susan George, p. 260.

10. Paul Boucher, in the *Guardian,* June 12, 1975, cited in Susan George.

11. Ho Kwon Ping, "Back to the Drawing Board," *Far Eastern Economic Review,* April 27, 1979, p. 87, citing a confidential World Bank report to the Intergovernmental Group on Indonesia.

12. Ibid.

13. Barry Newman, "Mixed Blessing: Do Multinationals Really Create Jobs in the Third World?" *Wall Street Journal,* Sept. 25, 1979, p. 1.

Question 7

1. *World Bank Annual Report 1979,* "Bank and IDA Cumulative Lending Operations, by Major Purpose and Region," (Washington: World Bank, June 30, 1979), p. 182.

2. World Bank, *Assault on World Poverty* (Baltimore: Johns Hopkins University Press, 1975), pp. 106, 118.

3. Ibid., p. 194.

4. *Credit Programs for Small Farmers in Latin America Can Be Improved,* A Report to the Congress by the Comptroller General of the United States, Dec. 9, 1977, p. 16.

5. Ibid., pp. 21-22.

6. Washington Office on Latin America, *The Nicaraguan AID Program: Rural Development Loan—INVIERNO* (Washington: WOLA, May, 1977), citing ATAK, *An Evaluation of AID Loan 524-T-031, INVIERNO* (ATAK, Oct. 1976), and INCAE (Harvard-

affiliated Business School), *INVIERNO, A Case Study* (Managua: INCAE, 1977), and interviews with Nicaraguan government officials.

7. Correspondence from Prof. Peggy Barlett, Emory University, to Mr. John Fasullo, Loan Officer, Costa Rica Commodity Systems Project, AID, Washington, 1979.

8. Comptroller General, *Credit Programs for Small Farmers...*, p. 18.

9. T.W.B. Cullen et al., "An Analysis of the Aid Debate," (draft) (Washington: World Bank, April 9, 1979), p. 24.

10. Milton Esman and Assoc., *Landlessness and Nearlandlessness in Developing Countries* (Ithaca, N.Y.: Center for International Studies, Cornell University, Feb. 15, 1978), p. 286.

11. Uma Lele, *The Design of Rural Development, A World Bank Research Publication* (Baltimore: Johns Hopkins University Press, 1975), pp. 204ff.

12. *Foreign Assistance and Related Programs Appropriations for 1980,* Part 2, International Financial Institutions, hearings before a House subcomm. of the Comm. on Approp., 96th Cong., 2nd Sess., pp. 191-192.

13. Ibid., p. 191.

14. See the World Bank news releases available from the Information and Public Affairs office of the World Bank, Washington, and the annual AID Congressional Presentations.

15. IDA News Release, No. 76/22 (Washington: World Bank, May 24, 1976).

16. Betsy Hartmann and James Boyce, *Needless Hunger: Voices from a Bangladesh Village* (San Francisco, Inst. for Food and Develop. Policy, 1979), pp. 48-50.

17. Ibid., pp. 49-50.

18. Per-Arne Stroberg, "Water and Development: Organizational Aspects of a Tubewell Irrigation Project in Bangladesh," mimeo, Dacca, March 1977.

19. Hartmann and Boyce, *Needless Hunger...*, pp. 49-50.

20. Stefan deVylder and Daniel Asplund, *Contradictions and Distortions in a Rural Economy: The Case of Bangla-desh* (Utredningsbyran: Policy Development and Evaluation Division, Swedish International Development Authority, n.d.), p. 161.

21. Per-Arne Stroberg, "Water and Development...."

22. Hartmann and Boyce, *Needless Hunger...,* p. 50.

23. Hugh Brammer, FAO, interview by staff of Inst. for Food and Develop. Policy, Dacca, Jan. 26, 1978.

24. See Tomasson Jannuzi and James Peach, *The Agrarian Structure of Bangladesh: An Impediment to Development* (Boulder, Colo.: Westview Press, 1980), for the most up-to-date survey of growing landlessness in Bangladesh.

25. World Bank, "Aide Memoir: Rural Development Project—IDA Credit," No. 631-BD (Washington: World Bank, Dec. 19, 1977), p. 1.

26. Quazi Kholiquzzaman Ahmad, "Rural Development in Bangladesh —Some Reflections on the Current Scenario," speech presented at the Second Annual Conference of Bangladesh Krishi Arthanitibeed Samity (Dacca: Bangladesh Institute of Development Studies, 1980).

27. World Bank, *Assault on World Poverty,* p. 143.

28. Ibid., p. 143.

29. We have received a number of communications (some anonymous) from Indonesia on peasant resistance to the imposition of this World Bank project.

30. Internal World Bank document (C18700/J23823/D2168 Annex 1).

31. Barry Newman, "Missing the Mark: In Indonesia, Attempts by World Bank to Aid the Poor Often Go Astray," *Wall Street Journal,* Nov. 10, 1977, p. 27.

32. *World Bank Annual Report 1978,* pp. 72-79.

33. Ernest Feder, *Lean Cows and Fat Ranchers: The International Ramifications of Mexico's Beef Cattle Industry* (Berlin: Research Institute of Berghof Stiftung for Conflict Research, n.d.), p. 32.

34. World Bank, *Assault on World Poverty,* p. 125.

35. *World Bank Annual Report 1978,* p. 28.

36. Cheryl Payer, "The World Bank and the Small Farmers," *Journal of Peace Research,* Vol. 16, No. 4 (1979), p. 299.
37. Operations Evaluations Dept., *Rural Development Projects: A Retrospective View of Bank Experience in Sub-Saharan Africa,* Report No. 2242 (Washington: World Bank, Oct. 13, 1978).
38. Ibid., p. 18.
39. Development Alternatives Inc., *Evaluation of Haiti Small Farmer Project* (Washington: Development Alternatives Inc., June 30, 1977).
40. Ibid., p. 51.
41. We have received a number of communications (some anonymous) from people in Haiti concerned about the impact of current U.S. aid programs. The quote comes from an informed observer whose name has been withheld.
42. Development Alternatives Inc., *Evaluation of Haiti Small Farmer Project,* pp. 114-115.
43. Cheryl Payer, "The World Bank and the Small Farmers."
44. Milton Esman, *Landlessness and Nearlandlessness in Developing Countries,* p. 111.
45. World Bank, *Rural Development,* Sector Policy Paper (Washington: World Bank, Feb., 1975), p. 21.
46. Cheryl Payer, "The World Bank and the Small Farmers," p. 300.
47. *LAAD Annual Report 1977.*
48. *LAAD Annual Report 1978.*
49. Jack Corbett and Ronald Ivey, *Evaluation of Latin American Agribusiness Development Corporation* (Washington: Checci and Co., July 31, 1974).
50. David Garino, "'Smart Money' Flows to Latin America, Aiming to Bolster Small Farm Businesses," *Wall Street Journal,* Feb. 12, 1975.
51. Corbett and Ivey, *Evaluation of Latin American Agribusiness Development Corporation* citing unofficial estimate from Lawrence Simon, Oxfam-America.
52. Checci and Co., *Evaluation of LAAD de Centroamerica* (Washington: Checci and Co., Nov. 23, 1977).
53. Ibid.
54. *LAAD Annual Report 1978.*
55. Overseas Private Development Corporation, *Annual Report 1977* and *Annual Report 1978* (Washington: Overseas Private Development Corporation).
56. World Bank, *Policy and Operations: The World Bank Group* (Washington: World Bank, Sept., 1974), p. 12. See also International Finance Corporation, *Annual Report 1978* (Washington: International Finance Corporation).
57. Frances Moore Lappé and Joseph Collins with Cary Fowler, *Food First: Beyond the Myth of Scarcity* (New York: Ballantine, 1979), pp. 286ff, 404.
58. World Bank, "Zaire—Appraisal of the Oil Palm Project," Report No. 1592-ZR (unpublished) (Washington: World Bank, March 29, 1978).
59. Ibid.

Question 8

1. For an exposition of this theory see World Bank, *Assault on World Poverty* (Baltimore: Johns Hopkins University Press, 1975), and World Bank, *Rural Development,* Sector Policy Paper (Washington: World Bank, 1975). See also *AID Congressional Presentations, Fiscal Years 1979* and *1980,* main volume.
2. Milton Esman and Assoc., *Landlessness and Nearlandlessness in Developing Countries* (Ithaca, N.Y.: Center for International Studies, Rural Development Committee, Cornell University, 1979). For an up-to-date study of landlessness in Bangladesh see Tomasson Jannuzi and James Peach, *The Agrarian Structure of Bangladesh An Impediment to Development* (Boulder, Colo.: Westview Press, 1980).
3. Gail Omvedt, American political economist living in Poona, India, forthcoming book on India. See also Frances Moore Lappé and Joseph Collins with Cary Fowler, *Food First: Beyond the Myth of Scarcity* (New York: Ballantine, 1979), Chapter 16, especially pp. 140-144.
4. International Labor Organization, *Poverty and Landlessness in Rural*

Asia (Geneva: International Labor Organization, 1977). See also the series of reports published by the United Nations Research Institute for Social Development (UNRISD) on the "green revolution." The series is available from the Reference Centre, UNRISD, Palais des Nations, Geneva.

5. J.S. Sarma and Shyamal Roy, "Behavior of Foodgrain Production and Consumption in India, 1960-1977," World Bank Staff Working Paper No. 339, July 1979, p. 28.

6. Ho Kwon Ping, "The Mortgaged New Society," *Far Eastern Economic Review,* June 29, 1979, citing the Asian Development Bank.

7. Phyllis Kim, "Saemaul Agriculture: South Korean Farmers Prop Up Export-Oriented Economy (Part I)," *AMPO: Japan-Asia Quarterly Review,* Vol. 12, No. 1 (1980), pp. 4-6.

8. Benedict Stavis, *Rural Local Government and Agricultural Development in Taiwan* (Ithaca, N.Y.: Rural Development Committee, Cornell University, 1974), p. 21.

9. *Asian Wall Street Journal,* Sept. 22, 1979.

10. Walden Bello and Severina Rivera, eds., *The Logistics of Repression and Other Essays* (New York and Washington: Friends of the Filipino People, 1977), pp. 80-82.

11. Filipino Information Service (FILINS) (P.O. Box 12215, San Francisco, CA 94112), No. 4, p. 2.

12. K. Das, "Mending Cracks in a Ricebowl" and Hugh Peyman, "The Ideals of a Showpiece" and "Of Rice and Anxious Men," *Far Eastern Economic Review,* Feb. 22, 1980, pp. 42-43.

13. Cheryl Payer, "The World Bank and the Small Farmers," *Journal of Peace Research,* Vol. 16, No. 4 (1979), pp. 303-304.

14. Department of Agriculture, *Farm Income Statistics,* Statistical Bulletin No. 547, July 1975; *Agricultural Statistics 1972;* and *1978 Handbook of Agricultural Charts* (Washington: U.S. Department of Agriculture).

15. Ronald Mighell and William Hoofnagle, comp., *Contract Production and Vertical Integration in Farming,* *1960 and 1970* (Washington: Economic Research Service, Department of Agriculture), p. 4. For 1970, the estimate given here is that 22 percent of U.S. food production is controlled directly or indirectly (through contracts) by processing corporations. In 1980, the proportion is more likely to be one-third, or greater. The American Agricultural Marketing Association has estimated that by 1985, three-quarters of all U.S. food production will be controlled by large corporations.

16. "Program of the Provisional Government of National Reconstruction of Nicaragua," *NACLA Report on the Americas,* Vol. 13, No. 5 (Sept.-Oct. 1979).

17. Frances Moore Lappé and Adele Beccar-Varela, *Mozambique and Tanzania: Asking the Big Questions* (San Francisco: Inst. for Food and Develop. Policy, 1980).

Question 9

1. *AID Policy on Agricultural Asset Distribution: Land Reform,* PD-72, approved and signed by Administrator John Gilligan, Jan. 16, 1979, quoting *1978 AID Agricultural Development Policy Paper.*

2. *Foreign Assistance and Related Programs Appropriations Fiscal Year 1980,* Part 1, hearings before the Senate Comm. on Approp., 96th Cong., 1st Sess., pp. 230-231.

3. Ibid., p. 231.

4. Frances Moore Lappé and Hannes Lorenzen, "Land Reform as Exploitation: Venezuela Peasants' Struggle," an interview with Venezuelan peasant Carlos Rojas (San Francisco: Inst. for Food and Develop. Policy, 1980).

5. M.R. Redclift, "The Influence of the Agency for International Development (AID) on Ecuador's Agrarian Development Policy," *Journal of Latin American Studies,* Vol. 2, No. 1 (1979), pp. 185-201.

6. World Bank, *Rural Development: Sector Policy Paper* (Washington: World Bank, 1975), p. 40.

7. Speech by World Bank President

Robert McNamara to the Board of Governors, Nairobi, Kenya, 1973.

8. World Bank, *Land Reform,* World Bank Paper—Rural Development Series (Washington: World Bank, 1974), p. 39.

9. Cheryl Payer, "The World Bank and the Small Farmers," *Journal of Peace Research,* Vol. 16, No. 4, (1979), p. 308.

10. Ibid., citing Rowton Simpson, "The New Land Law in Malawi," *Journal of Administration Overseas,* Vol. 6, No. 4 (1967).

11. Ibid., citing Montague Yudelman, *Africans on the Land* (Cambridge: Harvard University Center for International Affairs, 1964).

Question 10

1. Shirley Hobbs Scheibla, "McNamara's Band Sours: Directors, Staff Critical of World Bank Operations," *Barrons,* Dec. 3, 1979, pp. 9ff.

2. Anonymous personal communication, 1979.

3. Barry Newman, "Missing the Mark. In Indonesia, Attempts by World Bank to Aid Poor Often Go Astray," *Wall Street Journal,* Nov. 10, 1977, p. 27.

4. "World Bank Agricultural Sector Operations Review, Indonesia," p. 19.

5. World Bank, *An Analysis of "The Aid Debate,"* (Washington: World Bank, April 9, 1979), p. 28.

6. *Foreign Assistance and Related Programs Appropriations for 1980,* Part 2, International Financial Institutions, hearings before a House subcomm. of the Comm. on Approp., 96th Cong., 1st Sess., p. 49.

7. Betsy Hartmann and James Boyce, *Bangladesh: Aid to the Needy?* International Policy Report (Washington: Center for International Policy, May 1978), p. 7.

8. *World Bank Annual Report 1978,* appendix F, p. 147.

Question 11

1. Morgan Guaranty Trust Co., "Coping with the Imbalance in International Payments," *World Financial Markets,* Jan. 1977, p. 1.

2. UNCTAD, *Money and Finance and Transfer of Real Resources for Development,* International Financial Cooperation for Development, Report by UNCTAD Secretariat, TD/188/Supplement, Feb. 1976, p. 32.

3. Abelardo Valdez (AID official), speech before the Center of Inter-American Relations, April 1978, cited in *International Bulletin,* May 22, 1978, p. 7.

4. *World Bank Annual Report 1978,* pp. 140-141, 160-161.

5. Dr. Irving Friedman, *The Emerging Role of Private Banks in the Developing World* (New York: Citicorp, 1977), see statistical appendixes.

6. Ho Kwon Ping, "Caught in the Oil-debt Trap," *Far Eastern Economic Review,* Oct. 19, 1979, p. 56, and *Business Week,* July 9, 1979.

7. Peter Bowden, *How Project Assistance Adds to Third World Woes,* Report: News and Views from the World Bank, November-December, 1979 (Washington: World Bank, 1979), pp. 3-4.

8. *AID Congressional Presentation, Fiscal Year 1980,* p. 19.

9. Cyrus Vance, former Secretary of State, "Foreign Assistance and U.S. Foreign Policy," speech before the National Convention of the League of Women Voters, May 1, 1978.

10. Thomas Esdall, "Business Lobbying Helps Aid Effort," *Baltimore Sun,* July 23, 1979, pp. 1ff.

11. Ibid.

12. Judith Tendler, *New Directions Rural Roads,* AID Program Evaluation Discussion Paper No. 2, March 1979 (Washington: Office of Evaluation, Bureau for Program and Policy Coordination, AID), p. 5.

13. "McNamara on the Largest Issue: World Economy," *New York Times,* April 2, 1978, p. E-2.

14. Cyrus Vance, former Secretary of State, *U.S. Aid Programs, Fiscal Year 1980,* statement before the House Foreign Affairs Comm., 96th Cong., 1st Sess., Feb. 5, 1979.

15. Thomas Esdall, "Business Lobbying Helps Aid Effort."

Question 12

1. AID, *U.S. Overseas Loans and Grants and Assistance from International Organizations, Obligations and Loan Authorizations, July 1, 1945-Sept. 30, 1978* (Washington: AID), p. 6.
2. James Reibel, "Food Aid to India," unpublished thesis (Mt. Airy Rd., Croton-on-Hudson, N.Y., 1975), p. 1.
3. J.S. Mann, "The Impact of Public Law 480 on Prices and Domestic Supply of Cereals in India," *Journal of Farm Economics*, No. 49 (Feb. 1969), p. 143.
4. Dan Morgan and Don Oberdorfer, "Impact of U.S. Food Heavy on South Korea," *Washington Post*, March 12, 1975, p. 1.
5. Ibid., p. 12.
6. Loren Fessler, *Population and Food Production in South Korea*, Fieldstaff Reports 22—2, East Asia Series (New York: American University Fieldstaff Inc., 1975).
7. Korean Catholic Farmers' Movement, *Report: Study about the Production Cost of Rice—1977* (Daeheungdon, Daejon: Korean Catholic Farmers' Movement), p. 189.
8. Morgan and Oberdorfer, "Impact of U.S. Food Heavy on South Korea," p. 1.
9. Leonard Dudley and Roger Sandilands, "The Side Effects of Foreign Aid: The Case of P.L. 480 Wheat in Colombia," *Economic Development Cultural Change*, Jan. 1975, pp. 331-332.
10. Ibid.
11. Melvin Burke, "Does 'Food for Peace' Assistance Damage the Bolivian Economy?" *Inter-American Economic Affairs*, No. 25 (1971), pp. 9, 17.
12. We have received a number of communications (some anonymous) from Americans working in Haiti. For a more thorough report of the role of U.S. food aid in Haiti see *Food Monitor*, No. 10 (May-June 1979), pp. 8-11.
13. General Accounting Office, *Disincentives to Agricultural Production in Developing Countries*, Report to the Congress (Washington: General Accounting Office, Nov. 26, 1975), p. 25.
14. W.L. Clayton, Asst. Secretary of State, testimony on H.R. 2211, Bretton Woods Agreement Act to House Comm. on Banking and Currency, 79th Cong., 1st Sess., March 9, 1945, pp. 275, 282.
15. Eldridge Haynes, testimony to Senate Comm. on Ag. and Forestry, *Policies and Operations under P.L. 480* (Washington: Government Printing Office, 1957), p. 395.
16. Dan Morgan, "Opening Markets, Program Pushes U.S. Food," *Washington Post*, March 10, 1975, p. A-1.
17. Ibid.
18. "U.S. Grain Arsenal," *NACLA's Latin America and Empire Report*, Vol. 9, No. 7 (Oct. 1975), p. 27.
19. Dan Morgan, "Impact of U.S. Food Heavy on South Korea," *Washington Post*, March 12, 1975.
20. Dan Morgan, "Opening Markets, Program Pushes U.S. Food."
21. Dan Morgan, "Impact of U.S. Food Heavy on South Korea."
22. "U.S. Grain Arsenal," *NACLA's Report*, p. 23.
23. Dan Morgan, *Merchants of Grain* (New York: Viking Press, 1979), pp. 280ff.
24. *AID Congressional Presentation, Fiscal Year 1980*, p. 128.
25. "U.S. Grain Arsenal," *NACLA's Report*, p. 14.

Question 13

1. Dan Morgan, "U.S. Holds Back Food Aid in Rights Review," *Washington Post*, Nov. 22, 1977.
2. *Washington Post*, November 22, 1977, cited in Roger Burbach and Pat Flynn, "Agribusiness in the Americas" (New York: Monthly Review, 1980), chapter 3.
3. Senate, Comm. on Ag., Nutrition and Forestry, *Future of Food Aid 1977*, 94th Cong. 2nd Sess., p. 131.
4. *New Directions for U.S. Food Assistance: A Report of the Special Task Force on the Operation of Public Law 480 to the Secretary of Agriculture as Mandated in the Food and Agriculture Act of 1977* (Washington:

Dept. of Agriculture, May 1978), pp. 834-884.

Question 14

1. Betsy Hartmann and James Boyce, *Needless Hunger: Voices from a Bangladesh Village* (San Francisco, Inst. for Food and Develop. Policy, 1979), pp. 45-48.
2. World Bank, *Bangladesh: Food Policy Review* (Washington: World Bank, 1977), p. 39.
3. Donald McHenry and Kai Bird, "Food Bungle in Bangladesh," *Foreign Policy*, Summer 1977, p. 74.
4. Betsy Hartmann and James Boyce, *Bangladesh: Aid to the Needy?* International Policy Report (Washington: Center for International Policy, May 1978), Vol. 4, No. 1, p. 5.
5. Joseph F. Stepanek, *Bangladesh—Equitable Growth?* (New York: Pergamon Policy Studies, 1979), p. 58.
6. McHenry and Bird, "Food Bungle in Bangladesh," p. 75.
7. Qazi Kholiquzzaman Ahmad, "Rural Development in Bangladesh—Some Reflections on the Current Scenario," paper presented at the Second Annual Conference of Bangladesh Krishi Arthanitibeed Samity, Dacca, Jan. 12-13, 1980, p. 4. Available from the Bangladesh Inst. for Develop. Studies, Dacca. (The five percent increase is based on constant 1972-73 dollars.)
8. Stefan deVylder and Daniel Asplund, *Contradictions and Distortions in a Rural Economy: The Case of Bangladesh* (Utredningsbyran: Swedish International Develop. Authority), p. 45.
9. McHenry and Bird, "Food Bungle in Bangladesh," p. 78.
10. Hartmann and Boyce, *Needless Hunger...*, p. 48.
11. World Bank, *Bangladesh Current Trends and Development Issues* (Washington: World Bank, Dec. 15, 1978), p. 87.
12. *Amnesty International Annual Report 1977* (London: Amnesty International Publications), pp. 169-173.
13. Michael Chinoy, "Dacca's Strongman Consolidates," *Far Eastern Economic Review*, Jan. 16, 1976.

14. deVylder and Asplund, p. 45.
15. *FAO Production Yearbook*, Vol. 32 (1978). Total grain production is 19.3 million metric tons and population is 79.9 million. This amounts to almost 1.5 pounds of rice daily per capita, or almost 2400 calories (using rice calorie equivalent).
16. James Sterba, "Bangladesh Wooing Business," *New York Times*, April 9, 1979.

Question 15

1. Tomasson Jannuzi and James Peach, *Report on the Hierarchy of Interests in Land in Bangladesh* (Washington: AID, Sept. 1977), p. 88.
2. Michael Scott, *Aid to Bangladesh: For Better or Worse?* an interview (San Francisco: Oxfam America and Inst. for Food and Develop. Policy, 1979), p. 8.
3. Cited in the *Far Eastern Economic Review*, May 19, 1978, p. 35.

Question 16

1. Hans Ott, "Ethiopia 1973-75," *IPRA Food Group Circular Letter*, No. 4 (Jan. 1978), Special Issue: Food Aid. (c/o Erklarung von Bern, Gartenhofstrasse 27, 8004 Zurich), pp. 36-40.
2. Ibid.
3. Michael Behr (Oxfam field representative), personal correspondence to Roger Newton, June 3, 1977, Ouagadougou, Upper Volta.
4. AID, *Report on Examination of the PL 480 Title II Emergency Food Program*, Audit Report No. 3-641-78-1, Area Auditor General, Africa (Nairobi, Kenya: AID, Oct. 6, 1977).
5. Alan Riding, "U.S. Food Aid Seen Hurting Guatemala," *New York Times*, Nov. 6, 1977.
6. "The Relationship Between P.L. 480 Food Distribution and Agricultural Development in Guatemala," edited interview with Roland Bunch and William Ruddell, *Antigua Guatemala*, Aug. 21, 1977.
7. Ibid.

Question 17

1. "World Hunger, Health and Refugee

Problems: Summary of Special Study Mission to Asia and the Middle East," Report prepared for the Senate subcomm. on health of Comm. on Labor and Public Welfare, and subcomm. on refugees and escapees of Comm. on the Judiciary, 94th Cong., 2nd Sess., Jan. 1976, p. 104.

Question 18

1. *AID Policy on Agricultural Asset Distribution: Land Reform*, PD-72 (Washington: AID, Jan. 16, 1979).
2. World Bank, *Land Reform, Rural Development Series* (Washington: World Bank, July 1974), p. 40.
3. Center for International Policy, *Foreign Aid: Evading the Control of Congress*, International Policy Report (Washington: Center for International Policy, Jan. 1977).
4. Cheryl Payer, *The Debt Trap: The IMF and the Third World* (New York: Monthly Review, 1974), p. ix.
5. Michael Moffitt, testimony before subcomm. on international trade, investment and monetary policy of the House Comm. on Banking, Finance and Urban Affairs, 96th Cong., 2nd Sess., Feb. 6, 1980.
6. Payer, *The Debt Trap*, chapters 1 and 2.
7. Ibid.
8. Patricia Weiss Fagen, *The Links between Human Rights and Basic Needs* (Washington: Center for International Policy, 1978), pp. 7ff.
9. Jose Carrizo,"Peru's Babies are Dying," *New York Times*, Aug 24, 1979.
10. Tim Atwater, "The International Monetary Fund and the Third World," *Hunger* (Washington: National Impact, Feb. 1980), citing Jose Carrizo, "Peru's Babies are Dying," *New York Times*, Aug. 24, 1979. For additional information and action suggestions write to Peru Solidarity, P.O. Box 3580, Grand Central Station, New York, N.Y. 10017.
11. Michael Moffitt, "Buddy, can you spare a dime?" *New Internationalist*, Nov., 1978, p. 19.
12. Bernard Nossiter, "New Pragmatism at the IMF," *New York Times*, Feb. 5, 1980, pp. D-1, D-10.
13. Payer, *The Debt Trap*.
14. AID, *Foreign Assistance Provided by the U.S. Government to Foreign Countries and International Organizations by Category and Country*, Annual Foreign Assistance Report, Part 2 (Washington: AID, revised March, 1979), Table I-A and Table II.
15. Walden Bello, Peter Hayes, and Lyuba Zarsky, "500-Mile Island: The Philippine Nuclear Reactor Deal," *Pacific Research*, Vol. 10, No. 1, p. 10.
16. Nicholas Burnett, "The Quiet Subsidy," *Inquiry*, Dec. 24, 1979, p. 15.
17. AID, *Foreign Assistance... by Category and Country*, p. 73.
18. Bello, Hayes, and Zarsky, "500-Mile Island...," p. 12.
19. Ibid., p. 11.
20. Burnett, "The Quiet Subsidy," p. 15.
21. *Eximbank Record*, Vol. 3, No. 2 (Aug. 1978), p. 4.
22. Burnett, "The Quiet Subsidy," p. 13.
23. Ibid.
24. Ibid., p. 14.
25. Comptroller General, *Stronger Emphasis on Market Development Needed in Agriculture's Export Credit Sales Program*, Report to the Congress, ID-80-01 (Washington: Office of the Comptroller General, Oct. 26, 1979), p. IV.
26. Ibid., p. 37.
27. *OPIC Annual Report 1978*, p. 14.
28. OPIC, *An Introduction to OPIC* (Washington: Overseas Private Investment Corporation, July 1971), p. 2.
29. OPIC, "Country List," brochure (Washington: OPIC, 1975).
30. *OPIC Annual Report 1978*, pp. 32-35.
31. Ibid., p. 17.
32. Center for International Policy, "OPIC: Insuring the Status Quo," *International Policy Report*, Vol. 3, No. 2 (Sept. 1977), p. 2.
33. OPIC, *Topics* (Washington: OPIC, June 1975), p. 4-a.
34. Ibid.
35. *The OPIC Amendments Act*, Report of the Senate Comm. on Foreign Relations on S. 297, 93rd Cong., 2nd Sess., pp. 15ff.

36. *AID Congressional Presentation, Fiscal Year 1979*, main volume, p. 139-W.

37. For a detailed analysis see Noam Chomsky and Edward Herman, *The Washington Connection and Third World Fascism: The Political Economy of Human Rights*, Vol. 1 (Boston: South End Press, 1979).

38. AID, *Foreign Assistance...by Category and Country*, and *Amnesty International Report 1979* (London: Amnesty International Publications, 1979).

39. Michael Klare, *Supplying Repression: U.S. Support for Authoritarian Regimes Abroad* (Washington: Inst. for Policy Studies, 1977), and *AID Congressional Presentation, Fiscal Year 1979*, main volume. For thorough documentation on the many channels of U.S. support in most of these countries see Center for International Policy, *Human Rights and the U.S. Foreign Assistance Program* (Washington: Center for International Policy, 1978).

40. Department of Defense, *Foreign Military Sales and Military Assistance Facts* (Washington: Department of Defense, Dec. 1979), p. 19.

41. Ibid., p. 21.

42. Ibid.

43. John Markoff and Christopher Pain, "Advice Without Consent: The U.S. Military Abroad," *Pacific Research*, Jan.-Feb. 1978, based on data from *Congressional Record* Dec. 7, 1977, "Table B—Human Rights Related Legislative Sanction on Specific Countries (1976-1977)," p. S-19421; Nancy Stein, "Response to FOIA on Special Forces Mobile Training Teams: Dept. of the Army, Sept. 26, 1975"; and Harry Amos, "The MAAGs Live On," *National Defense*, Nov.-Dec. 1977, p. 233.

44. Department of Defense, *Foreign Military Sales and Military Assistance Facts*, p. 1.

45. Ibid.

46. Ibid.

47. Michael Klare, interview by staff of the Inst. for Food and Develop. Policy, April 23, 1980.

48. Department of Defense, *Foreign Military Sales and Military Assistance Facts*, pp. 1-3.

49. Ibid.

50. Ibid., pp. 7-12.

51. Ibid., pp. 1, 7.

52. *AID Congressional Presentation, Fiscal Year 1979*, main volume, pp. 139-140.

53. Klare, *Supplying Repression...*, pp. 18ff.

54. Ibid., pp. 25ff.

55. Ibid., p. 43.

56. Ibid., pp. 44-45.

57. Klare, interview, April 23, 1980.

58. Ibid.

59. Coalition for a New Foreign and Military Policy, *International Human Rights and the Administration's Security Assistance Program for Fiscal Year 1979*, Nicaragua (Washington: Coalition for a New Foreign and Military Policy, March 1978), p. 2.

60. Center for International Policy, *Human Rights and the U.S. Foreign Assistance Program: FY 1978*, Part 2—East Asia (Washington: Center for International Policy), p. 35.

Question 19

1. Mark Winiarski, "CRS: Image vs. Reality I: Morale, Funding Woes Hit Catholic Relief," *National Catholic Reporter*, Vol. 15, No. 42 (Sept. 28, 1979), pp. 18ff. This is the first of a three-part series exploring the operations of CRS.

2. Economic Development Bureau, *Appropriate Technology for Grain Storage* (New Haven, Conn.: Economic Development Bureau). For a general description of the work of the EDB, see "Alternative Consultants to Third World Countries" available from the same address.

3. To contact Gonoshasthaya Kendra, write to: P.O. Box Nayarhat, District

Dacca, Bangladesh. For a detailed evaluation of the work of Gonoshasthaya Kendra see: "Manzoor Ahmed, The Savar Project: Meeting the Rural Health Crises in Bangladesh" (Essex, Conn.: International Council for Educational Development, Oct. 1977).

4. To contact BRAC, write to: Bangladesh Rural Advancement Comm., 3 New Circular Road, Maghbazar, Dacca 17, Bangladesh. For a detailed evaluation of BRAC's programs see: "Manzoor Ahmed, BRAC: Building Human Infrastructures to Serve the Rural Poor" (Essex, Conn.: International Council for Educational Development).

5. Lutfur Rahman, "Case Study of Atgaon Landless Cooperative Society" (Dacca: Bangladesh Rural Advancement Comm., Jan. 4, 1978).

RESOURCES

Working alone it is hard to make a difference. A good way to support the initiatives of third world people for their own self-directed development is to work with groups that are 1) educating others about the impact of U.S. policies, 2) trying to influence those policies affecting third world people, and 3) responding directly to requests for support from those organizing for change in the third world. We have included a list of some of these groups. We know it is not exhaustive. Please write to us with additions and corrections.

Suggested Periodicals

Africa News, P.O. Box 3841, Durham, NC 27702, $25/yr.

Asia Monitor, Published by Asia Monitor Resource Center, 2 Man Wan Road, 17-C, Kowloon, Hong Kong, $10/yr.

Food Monitor, 350 Broadway, Suite 209, New York, NY 10013, $10/yr.

Multinational Monitor, published by the Corporate Accountability Research Group, P.O. Box 19312, Washington, DC 20036, $15/yr.

LADOC, publication of Latin American Documentation—USCC, 1312 Massachusetts Ave. N.W., Washington, DC 20005, $6/yr.

New Asia News, and *AMPO,* Japan-Asia quarterly review, published by Pacific-Asia Resource Center, P.O. Box 5250, Tokyo International, Japan.

New Internationalist, 113 Atlantic Ave., Brooklyn, NY 11201, $19/yr.

Southern Africa published by the Southern Africa Committee, 17 West 17th Street, New York, NY 10011, $10/yr.

Sugar World, a newsletter on issues of concern to sugar workers, published by GATT-Fly, 11 Madison Ave. Toronto, Ontario, Canada M5R 2S2, $10/yr.

Support Groups

General Organizations

Africa Resource Center, 464 19th Street, Oakland, CA 94612, 415/763-8011.

American Committee on Africa, 198 Broadway, New York, NY 10038, 212/962-1210.

American Friends Service Committee, 1501 Cherry Street, Philadelphia, PA 19102, 215/241-7000. Publication: *The Quaker Service Bulletin,* $5/yr.

Amnesty International of the U.S.A., 304 West 58th Street, New York, NY 10019, 212/582-4440. Publications: *Amnesty Action* and *Matchbox,* $15/yr.

Amnesty International Canadian Section, P.O. Box 6033, 2101 Algonquin Avenue, Ottawa, Ontario, Canada K2A 1T1.

Caribbean Basin Report, P.O. Box 1323, Station B, Ottawa, Ontario, Canada KIP 5R4, 613/226-7547. Publication: *Caribbean Basin Report,* $9/yr.

Center for the Progress of Peoples, 48 Princess Margaret Road, 1st Floor, Kowloon, Hong Kong. Publication: *Newsletter,* $3.50/yr. outside of Asia, $2/yr. in Asia.

Economic Development Bureau, P.O. Box 1717, New Haven, CT 06511, 203/776-9084.

Institute for Policy Studies, 1901 Q Street N.W., Washington, DC 20009, 202/234-9382.

Liberation Support Movement Information Center, P.O. Box 2077, Oakland, CA 94604, 415/655-5311. Publication: *APOYO,* $1 each.

Middle East Research and Information Project, P.O. Box 3122, Columbia Heights Station, Washington, DC 20010, 202/667-1188. Publication: *MERIP Reports,* $14/yr.

North American Congress on Latin America, 151 West 19th Street, 9th Floor, New York, NY 10011, 212/989-8890. Publication: *NACLA Report,* $13/yr.

Oxfam-America, 302 Columbus Avenue, Boston, MA 02116, 617/247-3304. Publication: *Oxfam News,* free.

People's Translation Service, 4228 Telegraph Ave., Oakland, CA 94609, 415/654-6725. Publication: *Newsfront International,* $22/yr.

Southeast Asia Resource Center, P.O. Box 4000-D, Berkeley, CA 94704, 415/548-2546. Publication: *Southeast Asia Chronicle,* $12/yr.

Southern Africa Media Center, California Newsreel, 630 Natoma Street, San Francisco, CA 94103, 415/621-6196. Educational films available for rent at flexible rates.

Washington Office on Africa, 110 Maryland Ave. N.E., Washington, DC 20002, 202/546-7961. Publication: *Washington Notes on Africa,* $5/yr.

Washington Office on Latin America, 110 Maryland Ave., N.E., Washington, DC 20002, 202/544-8045. Publication: *Latin America Update,* $10/yr.

By Country

Chile

Chile Committee for Human Rights, 2121 Decatur Place, N.W., Washington, DC 20008. Publication: *Newsletter,* donation requested.

Chile Legislative Center, 201 Massachu-

setts Ave. N.E., #201, Washington, DC 20002, 202/889-4670.

Non-Intervention in Chile, 151 West 19th Street, #905, New York, NY 10011, 212/989-5695. Publication: *Chile Action Bulletin,* donation requested.

Office for Political Prisoners and Human Rights in Chile, Box 40605, San Francisco, CA 94140, 415/285-5929, or 156 5th Ave., #521, New York, NY 10010, 212/749-7744. Publication: *Chile Today,* donation requested.

El Salvador

Casa El Salvador, P.O. Box 31424, San Francisco CA 94110, 415/282-3070. Write for literature list.

Committee in Solidarity with the People of El Salvador (CISPES), P.O. Box 12056, Washington, DC 20005, 202/887-5019. *El Salvador Alert!* ($5/6 months). Write for literature.

Inter-Religious Task Force on El Salvador, 475 Riverside Dr., Room 1020, New York, NY 10115, 212/870-3014. Write for literature.

Guatemala

Guatemala News and Information Bureau, P.O. Box 4126, Berkeley, CA 94704, 415/835-0810. Publication: *Guatemala!,* $7/yr.

Haiti

Union Patriotique Haitienne, 3900 Yuma Street N.W., Washington, DC 20016, 202/362-4743.

Indonesia (Timor)

U.S. Campaign for the Release of Indonesian Political Prisoners (TAPOL-USA) P.O. Box 609, Montclair, NJ 07042.

Philippines

Anti-Martial Law Coalition, P.O. Box 23644, Oakland, CA 94623. Publication: *Paliba,* free.

International Association of Filipino Patriots, P.O. Box 24737, Oakland, CA

94623. Publication: *Philippine Liberation Courier,* $8/yr.

Philippine Solidarity Network, 707 Wisconsin Street, San Francisco, CA 94107, San Francisco, CA 94107, 415/285-0395.

Union of Democratic Filipinos, P.O. Box 2759, Oakland, CA 94602, 415/482-3400. Publication: *Ang Katipunan,* $7.50/yr.

South Korea

North American Coalition for Human Rights in Korea, 475 Riverside Drive, #1538, New York, NY 10115, 212/678-6260. Publication: *Korea/Update,* donation requested.

Taiwan

The International Committee for the Defense of Human Rights in Taiwan—U.S.A., P.O. Box 5205, Seattle WA 98105, 206/527-4529. Publication: *Taiwan Communique,* $10/yr.

Thailand

Thai Information Center, P.O. Box 8995, Los Angeles, CA 90008. Publication: *TIC News.*

ABOUT THE INSTITUTE

The Institute for Food and Development Policy, publisher of this book, is a nonprofit research and education center. The Institute works to identify the root causes of hunger and food problems in the United States and around the world and to educate the public as well as policymakers about these problems.

The world has never produced so much food as it does today—more than enough to feed every child, woman, and man as many calories as the average American eats. Yet hunger is on the rise, with more than one billion people around the world going without enough to eat.

Institute research has demonstrated that the hunger and poverty in which millions seem condemned to live is not inevitable. Our Food First publications reveal how scarcity and overpopulation, long believed to be the causes of hunger, are instead symptoms—symptoms of an ever-increasing concentration of control over food-producing resources in the hands of a few, depriving so many people of the power to feed themselves.

In 55 countries and 20 languages, Food First materials and investigations are freeing people from the grip of despair, laying the groundwork—in ideas and action—for a more democratically controlled food system that will meet the needs of all.

An Invitation to Join Us
Private contributions and membership dues form the financial base of the Institute for Food and Development Policy. Because the Institute is not tied to any government, corporation, or university, it can speak with a strong independent voice, free of ideological formulas. The success of the Institute's programs depends not only on its dedicated volunteers and staff, but on financial activists as well. All our efforts toward ending hunger are made possible by membership dues or gifts from individuals, small foundations, and religious organizations. We accept no government or corporate funding.

Each new and continuing member strengthens our effort to change a hungry world. We'd like to invite you to join in this effort. As a member of the Institute you will receive a 25 percent discount on all Food First books. You will also receive our triannual publication, *Food First News*, and our timely Action Alerts. These Alerts provide information and suggestions for action on current food and hunger crises in the United States and around the world.

All contributions to the Institute are tax deductible.

To join us in putting Food First, just clip and return the attached form to the Institute for Food and Development Policy, 1885 Mission Street, San Francisco, CA 94103, USA.

☐ Yes, I want to ensure that the Institute for Food and Development Policy continues to be an independent and effective voice in the struggle against hunger and food problems. I have enclosed my tax-deductible contribution of:

☐ $20   ☐ $35   ☐ $50   ☐ Other $_____

☐ Please send me more information about the Institute, including your publications catalog.

Name _____

Address _____

City _____ State _____ Zip _____ Country _____

Institute for Food and Development Policy
145 Ninth Street
San Francisco, CA 94103 USA
(415) 864-8555

INSTITUTE
PUBLICATIONS

Now We Can Speak: A Journey through the New Nicaragua features interviews with Nicaraguans from every walk of life telling how their lives have changed since the 1979 overthrow of the Somoza dictatorship. Frances Moore Lappé and Joseph Collins, 124 pages with photographs.   *$4.95*

What Difference Could a Revolution Make? Food and Farming in the New Nicaragua provides a critical yet sympathetic look at the agrarian reform in Nicaragua since the 1979 revolution and analyzes the new government's successes, problems, and prospects. Joseph Collins and Frances Moore Lappé, with Nick Allen, 185 pages.   *$5.95*

Trading the Future: Farm Exports and the Concentration of Economic Power in Our Food System is a scholarly investigation which develops a comprehensive analysis of U.S. farming and food systems. It demonstrates how the increasing concentration of control over farmland, rapid erosion of soil, loss of water resources, and our growing reliance upon a narrow range of export crops parallels the process of underdevelopment experienced in the third world. Alterations in America's farm landscape threaten us not only with severe imbalances in control over resources, but also with rising prices in the midst of huge surpluses. James Wessel with Mort Hantman, 250 pages.
$8.95.

Diet for a Small Planet: Tenth Anniversary Edition, an updated edition of the bestseller that taught Americans the social and personal significance of a new way of eating. Frances Moore Lappé, 432 pages with charts, tables, resource guide, recipes, Ballantine Books.   *$3.50*

Food First: Beyond the Myth of Scarcity, 50 questions and responses about the causes and proposed remedies for world hunger. Frances Moore Lappé and Joseph Collins, with Cary Fowler, 620 pages, Ballantine Books, revised 1979.   *$3.95*

Comer es Primero: Mas Alla del Mito de la Escasez is a Spanish-language edition of *Food First*, 409 pages, Siglo XXI—Mexico.   *$9.95*

Food First Comic, a comic for young people based on the book *Food First: Beyond the Myth of Scarcity*. Leonard Rifas, 24 pages.   *$1.00*

Aid as Obstacle: Twenty Questions about our Foreign Aid and the Hungry demonstrates that foreign aid may be hurting the very people we want to help and explains why foreign aid programs fail. Frances Moore Lappé, Joseph Collins, David Kinley, 192 pages with photographs.   *$5.95*

Development Debacle: The World Bank in the Philippines, uses the World Bank's own secret documents to show how its ambitious development plans actually hurt the very people they were supposed to aid—the poor majority. Walden Bello, David Kinley, and Elaine Elinson, 270 pages with bibliography and tables.   *$6.95*

Against the Grain: The Dilemma of Project Food Aid is an in-depth critique which draws extensively from field research to document the damaging social and economic impacts of food aid programs throughout the world. Tony Jackson, 132 pages, Oxfam—England. *$9.95*

World Hunger: Ten Myths clears the way for each of us to work in appropriate ways to end needless hunger. Frances Moore Lappé and Joseph Collins, revised and updated, 72 pages with photographs. *$2.95*

El Hambre en el Mundo: Diez Mitos, a Spanish-language version of *World Hunger: Ten Myths* plus additional information about food and agriculture policies in Mexico, 72 pages. *$1.45*

Needless Hunger: Voices from a Bangladesh Village exposes the often brutal political and economic roots of needless hunger. Betsy Hartmann and James Boyce, 72 pages with photographs. *$3.50*

Circle of Poison: Pesticides and People in a Hungry World documents a scandal of global proportions, the export of dangerous pesticides to Third World countries. David Weir and Mark Schapiro, 101 pages with photos and tables. *$3.95*

Circulo de Veneno: Los Plaguicidas y el Hombre en un Mundo Hambriento is a Spanish-language version of *Circle of Poison*, 135 pages, Terra Nova—Mexico. *$3.95*

Seeds of the Earth: A Private or Public Resource? examines the rapid erosion of the earth's gene pool of seed varieties and the control of the seed industry by multinational corporations. Pat Roy Mooney, 126 pages with tables and corporate profiles. *$7.00*

A Growing Problem: Pesticides and the Third World Poor, a startling survey of pesticide use based on field work in the Third World and library research. This comprehensive analysis also assesses alternative pest control systems. David Bull, 192 pages with charts, photos, and references. *$9.95*

What Can We Do? An action guide on food, land and hunger issues. Interviews with over one dozen North Americans involved in many aspects of these issues. William Valentine and Frances Moore Lappé, 60 pages with photographs. *$2.95*

Mozambique and Tanzania: Asking the Big Questions looks at the questions which face people working to build economic and political systems based on equity, participation, and cooperation. Frances Moore Lappé and Adele Negro Beccar-Varela, 126 pages with photographs. *$4.75*

Casting New Molds: First Steps towards Worker Control in a Mozambique Steel Factory, a personal account of the day-to-day struggle of Mozambique workers by Peter Sketchley, with Frances Moore Lappé, 64 pages. *$3.95*

Agrarian Reform and Counter-Reform in Chile, a firsthand look at some of the current economic policies in Chile and their effect on the rural majority. Joseph Collins, 24 pages with photographs. *$1.45*

Research Reports. "Land Reform: Is It the Answer? A Venezuelan Peasant Speaks." Frances Moore Lappé and Hannes Lorenzen, 17 pages. *$1.50*

"Export Agriculture: An Energy Drain." Mort Hantman, 50 pages.   *$3.00*

"Breaking the Circle of Poison: The IPM Revolution in Nicaragua." Sean L. Swezey and Rainer Daxl, 23 pages.   *$4.00*

Food First Curriculum Sampler offers a week's worth of creative activities to bring the basics about world hunger and our food system to grades four through six. 12 pages.   *$1.00*

Food First Slideshow/Filmstrip in a visually positive and powerful portrayal demonstrates that the cause of hunger is not scarcity but the increasing concentration of control over food producing resources, 30 minutes.

$89 (slideshow), *$34* (filmstrip)

Write for information on bulk discounts.

All publications orders must be prepaid.

Please include shipping charges: 15% of order for U.S. book rate or foreign surface mail, $1.00 minimum. California residents add sales tax.

Food First Books

Institute for Food and Development Policy
1885 Mission Street
San Francisco, CA 94103 USA
(415) 864–8555

Frances Moore Lappé has been studying and writing about world food problems since 1969. In 1975 she founded the Institute for Food and Development Policy with Joseph Collins. She has written dozens of articles which have appeared in such diverse publications as *Harpers, The Nation, Parent's Magazine, Chemistry, New York Times,* and *Le Monde Diplomatique.* Her research has taken her to Mexico, Guatemala, the Philippines, Tanzania, and Mozambique. Presently she is investigating the impact of export-oriented agriculture and the growing number of agricultural imports in the United States.

Joseph Collins has lived, researched, and traveled extensively in Asia, Africa and Latin America during the past twenty years. He completed his doctoral studies at Columbia University and the Institute for Policy Studies. He collaborated with Richard Barnet and Ronald Mueller in researching *Global Reach: The Power of the Multinational Corporation.* His articles on development issues have appeared in numerous scholarly and popularly styled publications around the world. A founder of the Institute for Food and Development Policy, he is presently collaborating on a critical assessment of Cuba's food system.

Before joining the Institute for Food and Development Policy, **David Kinley** researched with two New York based organizations, focusing on the impact of U.S. multinational corporations in Latin America and the Caribbean, and on the concentration of control over major U.S. corporations. At the Institute his research has focused on the impact of U.S. government-funded aid programs in the third world. Field research has taken him to Guatemala, West Africa, and throughout Asia. He contributed as a research assistant for the revised edition of *Food First: Beyond the Myth of Scarcity* (Ballantine, 1979) with Lappé and Collins, and with them has written articles on the impact of U.S. aid programs on the hungry which have appeared in the *Los Angeles Times, Food Monitor, Christianity and Crisis,* and the *Progressive.* Presently he coordinates the Institute's Aid Education Project.